# GLIMPSES OF GOD

## Elaine J. Clinger Sturtz

*Illustrated by Lois Beery*

*With Illustrations by*
*Steve Fisher and Eva Wolfram*

Elaine J. Clinger Sturtz
Publisher

FIRST EDITION
Copyright © 1996 by
Elaine J. Clinger Sturtz

Hymn "Child of Blessing" words © 1981 Ronald S. Cole-Turner are reprinted with permission.

Some scripture quotations are from the *Revised Standard Version of the Bible,* copyrighted 1946, 1952 (c), 1971,1973, by the Division of Christian Education of the National Council of the Churches of Christ in the USA. Used by permission.

Library of Congress Catalog Card Number: 95-92690

ISBN 0-7880-0648-7     PRINTED IN U.S.A.

## Dedication

In loving memory of my grandson, Jonathan Craig, "J.C.", an angel who touched my heart with God's love and opened my eyes to see glimpses of God.

A special thank you to my husband, Dave, for his love, support and encouragement.

Thank you to all the people through whom I have seen God and who helped to inspire this book.

# Table of Contents

# Introduction

God is real! God is everywhere. Look and let your mind's eye reveal to your heart the wondrous things God allows: mountains that are snow capped, streams of water cascading over rocks, trees and flowers that cause you to gasp in wonderment, sunrises and sunsets that stop you in your footsteps. All these things are ours to see, feel, hear and touch.

But the greatest wonder of all is the glimpses of God you see all around you. Wherever you are, stop and look at the faces, old, young, pretty and not so handsome, wrinkled, and smooth. In these glimpses you will surely see God's magnificent work.

Open your heart and be willing to be showered with God's grace and His willingness to allow us to see in each other what He desires, glimpses of Himself right in our midst.

# Chapter 1

# Grandma

*"Life is what we make it to be with God's help."*
                                    *— Grandma*

# The Beginning Of Faith

**Scripture**
**I am reminded of your sincere faith, a faith that dwelt first in your grandmother Lois and your mother Eunice and now, I am sure, dwells in you.**                    - 2 Timothy 1:5

I looked through the window on the door before I knocked and there she sat, in her favorite chair, holding her leather Bible. I knocked and she looked up, smiled and gently placed her precious Bible lovingly on the table under a beautiful antique lamp which always beamed light into the living room of my Grandma's home. The light reflected on the Bible and expressed to me so vividly the greater Light my grandmother received from her daily reading of God's Word.   Grandma's life reflected the light and love of Jesus Christ.

Grandma was never one to preach her faith but to live her faith. As a child, I was fascinated with Grandma's love of the Church and her patience and care for each family member. I invariably wondered how she could love and accept people when they had wronged her or said or done something unkind. She constantly found the good in everyone. She said that is what God's Word taught her to do.

As an adolescent and a teenager, when I was allowed to ride my bike into town I did not go play with my friends, go to the Dairy Snack for ice cream or to the toy store or candy store; I went to Grandma's house. It was a small, white, framed house with a little yard in front and back, but it was the richest and most beautiful house to me because it was filled with the greatest treasure, my grandmother and her love!

She believed in me more than I believed in myself. I believe she saw herself in me and wanted to nurture  the seed God had planted in me. Grandma in her wisdom and closeness with God saw within me what the Lord had planned for my life even before I ever knew His purpose and direction for my life. Grandma was so close to her Heavenly Father and walked so continuously in His holy presence that she heard God speak to me and call me.

As I matured and began to believe and accept God's call in my life, I still lacked the confidence in myself, but Grandma always believed and knew where God was leading me. She continually encouraged me in the Lord and in the right direction. She knew God would grant to me the necessary skills and eventually build my confidence to trust in God and turn my life over to the leading hand of God.

I have learned much about faith and what it means to trust God through the reading and re-reading of my grandmother's letters and reflecting on her life and on her peaceful death.

I believe the faith of Grandma is alive through me. She continues to give me guidance and strength to face each day, and I believe she is my "guardian angel" who leads and protects me. Each day I look into the eyes of my grandmother through the picture of her which sits next to her rocking chair in our bedroom, and it gives me the assurance of God's presence with me through my grandmother.

The love we have for special people never dies when their earthly bodies leave this world, and we can no longer touch them with our physical hands. I believe they touch our hearts forever with their love and inner guidance as we remember the things they taught us and how they lived their lives. What we remember about our loved one that made the person special can live on in us. Our faith grows and matures as we pass it on to others.

Therefore, the faith that began in my grandmother continues to live through me.

**Prayer**

Loving Father, thank You for the gift of special people who touch my life with their love. Guide me in sharing that love with others so that their love and faith will live on forever in the hearts of those on earth. Amen.

# Grandma's Comforter

**Scripture**
**Oh to be safe under the shelter of thy wings!**      - Psalm 61:4

**Comfort, comfort my people, says your God.**      - Isaiah 40:1

**He will cover you with his pinions, and under his wings you will find refuge; his faithfulness is a shield and buckler.**
                                                      - Psalm 91:4

**Blessed be the God and Father of our Lord Jesus Christ, the Father of mercies and God of all comfort, who comforts us in all our affliction, so that we may be able to comfort those who are in any affliction, with the comfort with which we ourselves are comforted by God.**      - II Corinthians 1:3-4

Sometimes I think I must be cold-blooded. When there is a chill in the air, it goes directly to my feet and my hands. After I preach on a Sunday morning my hands are so cold that the first ten people who shake my hand receive a cold shock. When I get cold at home, I like to wrap up in a blanket or snuggle under the comforter in the bed.

I have a very special comforter, though some may call it a quilt. Every stitch in it was sewn with love by the hands of my grandmother. My grandmother called them comforters, and I now know the reason. Yes, they keep you warm in the cold of winter with a blanket sewn in the middle, but they also give you comfort knowing you are wrapped in a blanket made with loving hands.

When I went to college and then to my first pastorate, my comforter went with me. I used it on my bed and even outside to lie on the grass. It received much usage. My grandmother made it just for me, and she made all of her grandchildren one just for them. Mine has a purple backing and each small square is hand sewn together with a knot in each corner. Every time I would feel lonely or homesick or just in need of a little love, I would cover up with my comforter and feel the warmth of my grandmother's love.

I am sure that as my grandmother made my comforter she thought of me and prayed for me with every stitch. She put her love into action and made a very special gift that I will always treasure. Her gift is an expression of her love and prayer that I will always be wrapped in the warmth of God's love.

One cold, snowy afternoon my husband, Dave, decided to lie down for a short nap and asked for a blanket. I went to the hall closet and saw one of my Grandmother's comforters. I took it off the shelf gently and almost reverently. As I covered Dave with the comforter, it looked so inviting I slipped under it, too, for a short nap and dreamed of Grandma wrapping her arms of love around me

God longs to wrap each one of us in the warmth of His love. God's arms are out-stretched to receive us and to wrap us in the comfort and warmth of His love.

**Prayer**

Loving God, thank You for always being here for me. When I am cold or lonely or feeling afraid and alone, thank You that You stretch out Your arms to bring me close to You and wrap me in Your love which warms me and comforts me. Thank You. Amen.

# Beets On The Ceiling

**Scripture**
**The Lord watch between you and me, when we are absent one from the other.** - Genesis 31:49

**Be watchful, stand firm in your faith, be courageous, be strong.**
- I Corinthians 16:13

In one of Grandma's letters to me she told me of the story of the beets: "I had quite a little excitement going on here in my kitchen. I was cooking some beets in my pressure cooker. I was in the bedroom working on a new comforter when all at once there was a loud bang in the kitchen. I rushed to see the air filled with beets, steam, etc., so thick I couldn't see through. I had always used a pressure cooker and never had trouble before. It had gone bad all at once. The walls, cabinets, and ceiling were well-covered with beets and juice. I commenced wiping up with paper toweling. Then I called Sandy and told her what had happened. She offered to help, but I said I would ask David to help when he came home to clean the ceiling. Carolyn stopped in at 10 o'clock while Nathan was at his Kindergarten. She got the ladder and cleaned for about 2 hours. Then David came in and cleaned more. I had washed and cleaned and picked up things off the floor in the meantime. The lid of the cooker went into the ceiling and made a hole.

"Of course I feel somewhat depressed but am so thankful I wasn't in the kitchen at that time or I could have been hurt. I give thanks every morning to God for his watchful care over me and all my loved ones."

There are times in all our lives that it seems something "blows up" in our face or around us. How do we handle it? What do we do? My grandmother gives us sound advice. First we face the

18

situation, doing what we personally can do and then call for help. Then we thank God for watching over us and helping us through the situation.

What a joy to know we are not alone in this world! God is truly with us and gives to us loved ones with whom to share our lives. In my family, when there is a need, there is always someone there to help. I believe God intended for all families to support one another. Unfortunately, not all families do. Therefore, even if you do not have a supportive family, you can reach out to your extended Christian family. No matter what, you always have the assurance that God is with you. You are never alone.

## Prayer

Lord, no matter what happens today, thank You for watching over me and always being with me. When life seems to fall apart around me, may I remember You are with me and give to me special people through whom you work to give me help. Thank you. Amen.

# Life In The Nursing Home

**Scripture**
**Whither shall I go from thy Spirit?  Or whither shall I flee
from thy presence?**                                    - Psalm 139:7

**Surely the Lord is in this place; and I did not know it.**
                                                        - Genesis 28:16

My grandmother lived alone for over twenty years in her little
white framed home.  She enjoyed visitors and time spent with
family, but she also enjoyed and wanted her privacy and time to
be alone.

When her health declined and necessitated the move into a
nursing home, it was quite an adjustment for the entire family
though Grandma seemed to take it in stride.  She did not want to
leave her home and especially her privacy and all her treasured
possessions.  The nursing home staff helped to accommodate her
wishes as much as possible with a private room and meals served
in her room even though she was capable of eating her meals in
the dining hall with the other residents.  Her room became her
little "apartment" and her "home away from home" with a few of
her treasured possessions neatly placed around her room.

Grandma usually kept her door closed so people would have
to knock on her door to come in just as in her house.  She made her
own bed and took her own bath as long as she was physically
capable.  She would walk down the hall just as she walked down
the sidewalk and visit friends and other residents. One month
Grandma was chosen as the "Resident of the Month" for the nursing home.  The nursing home newsletter told details of Grandma's
life and her family.  The article concluded with these words
from Grandma:

"I wish to thank the staff of the Manor (Nursing Home) and all my family and friends for their love and kindness, and to thank God for his love and guidance all through my life."

Yes, Grandma was thankful. She was in a place where she did not want to be and surrounded by people not of her choice, but she was still thankful. Grandma was thankful to God for His purpose and plan for her life even when His plan was different from her desires. Grandma knew that no matter where she was, God was with her.

God is with us wherever we are and in whatever we are doing. God will never forsake us or leave us alone to falter by ourselves. God's Spirit is with us wherever we go. When we find ourselves in a place that we do not want to be, but God has brought us to this place, thank God for his presence and know God has a plan and a reason for our being here. Just trust Him.

**Prayer**

God, there are times when I want to question You and Your plan for my life, but help me to trust Your guidance and to know You are with me wherever I go. Thank you, Lord, for Your presence. I cannot make it without You. Amen.

# Cookie Kind Of Love

**Scripture**
**I have given you an example, that you also should do as I have done to you.** - John 13:15

**For to this you have been called, because Christ also suffered for you, leaving you an example, that you should follow in his steps.** - 1 Peter 2:21

As I took the last dozen cookies out of the oven and placed them on the wax paper to cool, I thought of how many dozens of cookies I had baked over the years. While I do have a sweet tooth and enjoy home-baked cookies, most of the cookies never touch my lips.

I enjoy baking cookies for other people. I keep my husband's office supplied with cookies every week or so, and my neighbors enjoy the sweet morsels.

"Why do you bake so many cookies?" I was once asked. While I have always enjoyed baking since I was a little girl, I know the real reason, because of my grandmother.

Grandma's cookie jar was never empty. No matter what time of day or year, Grandma made sure there was a cookie or two just for you. Everyone in the family headed to the cookie jar whenever we visited Grandma. It was her gift of love to each one of us. Her love, as well as her cookie jar, was never empty.

I bake and give away cookies because of the loving memory of Grandma who taught me there is more in a cookie than the ingredients. There is the gift of love. Her cookie jar expressed her love, it was always there, never empty and only the best.

Baking cookies has become a natural part of my life as well as sharing them and the love that goes with them with others. As I think about these cookies, I have to ask myself, "What else have I learned from Grandma that has now become a natural part of my life?"

Grandma taught me to live my faith daily, to look on the bright side of life by being positive, to find the good in everyone and every situation. But most of all she taught me about Christ and His love by living her faith. Grandma always believed in me and always expected the best of me. No matter what happened, she always loved me. All this and cookies, too.

We can learn how to live our lives to the fullest through the example of other people around us if we will take the time to listen and follow their guidance. Jesus Christ is our true example to follow. Therefore, as we look to others for guidance, we need to ask, "Who is following Christ?"

There are people right now who are watching you and following your example. Does your life radiate the light and love of Christ?

**Prayer**

Thank You, Lord, for the gift of Grandmothers and how they express Your love. Keep me open to learning from Your saints and to pass on Your love to others. Amen.

# Patriotism Of A Matriarch

**Scripture**
**Render therefore to Caesar the things that are Caesar's, and to God the things that are God's.** - Matthew 22:21

**You shall love the Lord your God with all your heart, and with all your soul and with all your mind.** - Matthew 22:37

"It is incumbent upon every person to contribute to his country's welfare," wrote my grandmother on the bottom of a piece of paper on which was also written an invocation Grandma gave at a DAR (Daughters of the American Revolution) function. I found my grandmother's prayer and inspiring thought in a book about the DAR which my Mom recently gave to me.

What a joy it was to read my grandmother's writing. It was like a letter from heaven to me.

The DAR was a wonderful organization in which Grandma joyfully participated, for she was proud of her heritage, to be a Daughter of one who had fought in the American Revolution. Within Grandma's heart was first her love of God, her love of family and her love of her country. She would often speak with thanksgiving for being born in a free country. She was proud that her son, my dad, had served in the military as well as her grandson, my brother.

One of the prayers I found, Grandma gave on Veteran's Day:

"Our Heavenly Father, we ask thy blessing upon our nation as we give thanks for this Veteran's Day which we are commemorating today. We give thanks for all blessings especially for the peace of God which we have in our hearts as Christians.

"We're grateful for thy providence in providing all the necessities of life, especially for the food of which we are about to partake. "May we ever be mindful of the needs of others around the world. In the name of Jesus Christ we pray. Amen."

These simple yet eloquent words of Grandma remind me how often I take for granted the privilege of living in this country and the blessings and the abundance of necessities I have at my disposal each day.

I am grateful to God each day for the blessings He has given to me, but I am also reminded of the responsibility I have to share these blessings with others. For I believe as my grandmother taught me, the more God blesses you with, the more responsibility you have to share these blessings with others.

**Prayer**

"O God, we thank thee for thy wisdom and strength which thou dost give us according to our needs. Continue we pray to lead our nation in wisdom, justice, and love until peace is established again in this world. For ourselves, may we continue in love and praise to thee. Amen." (Grandma)

# Chapter 2

# J.C. : The Angel
Of God

*"I am thankful for the lives of all my grandchildren."*

*— Grandma*

*He gave so much*
*To be so little*
*But angels always do.*

*— Quote on*
*J.C.'s Grave*

# His Purpose In Life

**Scripture**
**We know that in everything God works for good with those who love him, who are called according to his purpose.**

- Romans 8:28

**... for thereby some have entertained angels unawares.**

- Hebrews 13:2

The hospital gave Dave and me special buttons that read "I'm A New Grandparent." The nurses on the floor made a special button for Christopher by covering the previous button with tape and writing "I'm A Big Brother."

Jonathan Craig came into the world surrounded by love, warmth, and a sense of wonder. He was my grandson "officially," as his mother told me, since he was born after I joined the family. Yes, he was truly mine, but family members claimed J.C. as "their special boy" for one reason or another.

In life, J.C. taught us how to laugh a little more, love a little more deeply and enjoy life a little more enthusiastically. He smiled a little longer and hugged a little tighter than most children do, and now I know why.

J.C. gave his love freely, unconditionally and without reservation each day of his short 11 month life. He loved life to the fullest he could as a little baby and tried to teach those around him to do the same through the only means he had, his bright happy smile and attitude.

On March 5, 1993, J.C. fulfilled God's purpose for his life on earth, and God's little angel went back to be with God. Some people achieve their purpose in 11 months while it takes other people 90 years. It is difficult to comprehend that a child's life ended so young, so incomplete with so much left undone, undiscovered and untouched by his little hands. He never spoke my name, never played baseball, never ran across a field of daisies, never..... If one dwells on what was not to be one will never be able to go on with life and live again. One life has ended here on earth, but we are still here to take up life where one ended.

Our thoughts must not dwell on the finality of life nor the sadness and sorrow, though one must face and go through the needed grief and arrive at the other side.

I realized I needed to contemplate what was J.C.'s purpose in life, and what did I personally learn from this young life that will help me to reach out to others in life and reach my own potential and purpose in life.

One purpose of J.C.'s life was to rekindle the childlike faith God calls all of us to have. In the Gospel of Matthew (18:1-4) Jesus blesses the children and tells the disciples and us that we must become like little children to enter the Kingdom of Heaven.

Jesus wants us to retain the childlike qualities of trust and faith. J.C.'s brother, Christopher, taught us through J.C.'s death the beauty and simplicity of a childlike faith, for Christopher knew and accepted that his brother was now in heaven with God. Though he missed his brother and cried tears of sadness, he knew that now God was taking care of an angel named J.C. He is in the loving arms of God where we all want to be.

J.C. taught us about unconditional love. A child loves without condition or prejudice, loving totally and completely. As we mature we reserve our love and share our love under certain conditions and circumstances. We are to love others with God's love, unconditional and with no strings attached.

Our attitude toward life is affected by how we love. J.C. was always happy even through the pain of ear infections and surgery for ear tubes. When he came out of surgery his eyes were happy as he stood in the baby bed with a bottle of apple juice in his mouth. He had a genuine smile that was contagious. Our attitude of love affects every part of our lives. The most important part of life is our love relationships. When everything else is stripped away, it is those we love that are most important.

An angel of God. Yes, God gave to us an angel for a short time

31

to touch our lives with a very special love that transcends time and place. He gave us the assurance of the unconditional love God has for us to spark within us the presence of God to share with others.

J.C.'s father, Craig, wrote the following tribute to J.C. the night following his death:

"In memory of Jonathan Craig Sturtz
born to us March 26, 1992

"Words cannot describe the love, hope and happiness he gave to all who knew him. God chose to take him March 5, 1993, for reasons we now cannot understand, but in faith and love for J.C., we will carry on through the pain and sorrow knowing he is in a far better home now with God.
"We truly love and will always miss our son, J.C. Sturtz, and to all who have lost such a joyful part of their lives, we share in your grief." — Craig David Sturtz

Each of us has a purpose in life designed by God, and it is fulfilled in God's time. J.C. not only taught us about love, but about ourselves and the need to change or to let go. J.C. brought his parents back together through the grief and sorrow and the need for support. His father has dedicated his life to J.C. and has begun to let go of a past that had torn his life apart.

When a loved one dies, the pain and grief at times become too much to bear and we want to shut out the world and just shut down our lives, but God calls us to do the very opposite of these emotions. God asks us what we have learned from this precious life of our loved one and how can we take what we have learned from our loved one to fulfill God's purpose for our own life.

Each morning as I walk down our stairs, I look into the smiling face of J.C. through his picture which hangs on the wall at the foot of our stairs. My heart aches for a moment to hold him in my arms, but then his smile is contagious and I smile, knowing God is truly with me and that J.C. is at home with God. J.C. is our little angel who watches over all of his family and leads us through his memory to share God and God's love with those around us.

Life is short. There is no time to hold grudges, to not forgive or to live in the past of "what if's." Live today, for that is all we have for the moment. Life is like a pie. We receive one piece at a time, never the whole pie. If you do not eat your piece of the pie, it will spoil. Just like in life. If you do not live each day to the fullest, it will waste away. Live each moment to the fullest. Remember those who have gone on before you and continue their work for God in this world.

**Prayer**

Merciful Father, I thank You for the special angel You gave to share Your love with me, even if only for a short time. May I be aware of the angels around me. Help me to live each day to the fullest, following Your purpose and plan for my life. Amen.

# Baptism

**Scripture**
**In those days Jesus came from Nazareth of Galilee and was
baptized by John in the Jordan.**          - Mark 1:9

**Go therefore and make disciples of all nations, baptizing them
in the name of the Father and of the Son and of the Holy Spirit.**
                                                    **- Matthew 28:19**

*"Jonathan Craig, I baptize you in the name of the Father, and
the Son, and the Holy Spirit. Amen."*

On July 12, 1992, I held in my arms our little grandson, Jonathan
Craig (J.C.), and I baptized him into the family of God along
with his brother, Christopher. What a joy to hold a precious angel,
a gift from God, and publicly declare him a child of God. As
a part of the worship service, the hymn "Child of Blessing,
Child of Promise" (written by Ronald S. Cole-Turner) was
sung by the entire Church Family to affirm the baptism. J.C.
was truly a child of God, an angel of love. The third verse of the
hymn reads

**"Child of joy, our dearest treasure,
God's you are, from God you came.
Back to God we humbly give you;
live as one who bears Christ's name."**

Little did I know as I held our grandson and we sang these
words that J.C. would return to live with God in heaven so soon.
In less than eight months, J.C. died and went back to heaven to
live as an angel of God.
I truly baptized one of God's angels, one of His littlest angels.

34

God gave to us J.C. for just a short period of time to teach us and to sacrifice his life for his family.

Tears flowed within my heart as I baptized J.C. They were tears of joy and of an awesome presence of God's Spirit resting upon God's little miracle.

Tears now fill my eyes at each baptism I have witnessed since the death of J.C. I cry through the special baptismal hymn and tears even fill my eyes now as I read again the words of the hymn and remember the special day of baptism.

I write these words on the six month anniversary of J.C.'s death, and my heart cries tears of sadness and loss. My arms ache to hold J.C. once more. My eyes swell with tears, longing just to see his smile. My ears strain to hear his baby noises. But he is not here; he will never be here again.

But baptism gives me hope in the midst of these tears. Baptism reminds me that we are all raised with Christ. We are each one of His children, a part of God's family. We belong to God. When the life we know here on earth ends, our life with God continues in heaven. Baptism, though, does not assure us our right to go to heaven; it is not a magical rite for entrance into heaven. Baptism is an outward sign that God has claimed this child as His very own without reservation or restrictions.

J.C.'s baptism gives me the satisfaction that outwardly everyone who witnessed the baptism knows that J.C. is a child of God. For me personally, J.C.'s baptism reminds me that for a moment I saw heaven's window open as I held God's precious miracle angel.

I may always cry at a baptism, but the tears assure me of the great love God has for one of His angels.

**Prayer**

Thank You God, for the gift of baptism which assures me that You have chosen us as Your very own children. May each baptism I witness bring me closer as Your Child. Amen.

# The Anniversary

**Scripture**
**O death, where is thy victory?  O death were is thy sting?**
- I Corinthians 15:55

**Jesus said, "I am the resurrection and the life; he who believes
in me, though he die, yet shall he live."**          - John 11:25

The day marked the anniversary.  There was no celebration, no
cards, no flowers of joy, no words of congratulations; only tears of
sorrow.  It was the anniversary of his death.

The day looked like an ordinary day.  Everyone around was
busy going to work, getting ready for school but in her mind she
remembered.  A lump stuck in her throat and she became nervous
at the thought of driving to school.  Today was the anniversary of
the accident where she almost died.

I jumped awake from a nightmare...again.  I looked around
trying to remember where I was.  I was safe in my home, and then
I remembered, today was the anniversary of the fire that destroyed
my childhood home.

Her birthday came and I bought a birthday card, but to what
address shall I mail it?  If I lay it on the table will she know that I
thought of her today?  Should I take her flowers?  Will she know I
care?  Today she has been in heaven for four years.

Anniversaries are not always times of joy and celebration.
There are anniversaries of sad times, deaths, and events in all our
lives which we will always remember when the date rolls around
each year.  It does not matter how long ago it has been, one or one
hundred years, the memory will always be there and the emotion
of the day may bring tears and sadness for a while.

How do we make it through these anniversaries every year?  I
have found that it is only through the grace of God and the gift of

prayer. Having the faith and assurance our loved one is with God helps bring healing to the anniversary. The day is also a time to remember the good times and good memories of the person or the memories before the disaster struck.

Anniversaries are a time to share with others the good memories and to find healing through sharing. We think about what we have learned from the person and how the person has helped us in our own life, and then we can give thanks to God for the gift of the person's life among us, knowing our lives will never be the same because of the touch of love given by our loved one.

When that anniversary rolls around for you, cry a few tears, say a prayer of thanksgiving to God for how your loved one touched your life, and then remember one thing you have learned from your loved one and pass it on. For when you remember and pass it on; you keep the memory of your loved one alive.

## Prayer

Lord, thank You for being with us in our sorrow and in our remembrances. Thank You for that special person in my life whom You gave to me for awhile and who is now with You. May I remember today with joy what I learned from my loved one and pass that love on to another. Amen.

# The Healing

**Scripture**
**Jesus said to him, "Do you want to be healed?"**          - John 5:6

**Come to me, all who labor and are heavy laden, and I will give you rest.**          - Matthew 11:28

The phone rings in the middle of the night. The voice on the other end is faint but familiar in the midst of the sobs. "I need you." "Where are you?" "I'll be right there."

The doorbell rings. You jump awake and glance at the clock, 2:32 A.M. Panic strikes.

You awake and walk slowly into her room. She opens her eyes slowly, looks up and gently speaks,"Today is the day." Tears flood your heart and overflow into your eyes. She knows.

The sun had been bright and warm all day. We had just come from a long walk, talking and unwinding on vacation. The phone rings, "J.C. has died." We are numb. Tears, questions, anger, prayer shoot through our minds like wild arrows as our hearts are torn apart. "We'll be there as soon as we can get a flight."

Death. Whenever it comes, you are never prepared. It comes so quickly and it lingers sometimes at the door for awhile, but it always comes.

Death is the final and perfect healing from this world. It is the only way to reach heaven, to go through death's unknown door. When loved ones are sick, we pray for healing to come to their bodies. We want a healing of their earthly bodies, but sometimes healing comes only through death.

When we pray we have a preconceived idea of what we want God to do, and when God does not answer our prayer the way we demand, we think no healing took place. We need to keep praying but leave the form of healing up to God. We cannot explain the reason for suffering and sickness, but we need to allow God to work through every situation. Sometimes healing comes through the perfect healing of death, and our loved one is given a new heavenly body which will have no more pain or sorrow.

When our grandson, J.C., died of an accident, there was no chance or opportunity to pray for his healing. He had already died and was with God. Prayer was still a part of the healing process. We had to pray for healing to our lives asking God to help pick up the pieces of our broken hearts and to take up life again without our special little angel among us.

The healing in death continues throughout our entire lives until we, too, experience the perfect healing in death. Healing continues within our hearts. We share wonderful memories of a short but influential life, acknowledging all that J.C. taught us and how we can share that love and blessing with others.

Letting go and taking up life is never easy. Time does not heal all wounds; only God's grace, love and forgiveness does. Only by leaning on the everlasting arms of God can we take up life again and find healing and wholeness in life again.

**Prayer**

Thank You, dear Father, for the gift of life and of love. May Your healing power of love enter my life and heart and bring me to wholeness and peace in Your loving arms. Amen.

# The Faith Of A Five-Year-Old

**Scripture**
**But Jesus said, "Let the children come to me, and do not hinder them; for to such belongs the kingdom of heaven."**
- Matthew 19:14

For six months after our grandson, J.C., died, his five-year-old brother, our grandson, Christopher, spent each weekday with me while his parents were at work.

Early in our time together, Christopher and I talked much about J.C. and his death. Like a normal five-year-old, Christopher had a lot of questions which needed answers, but he also had a very simple yet strong childlike faith that sustained him.

Christopher had just arrived at the babysitter's home from kindergarten as his little brother choked to death. He saw some of what happened to his brother, and Christopher continued to be a part of all that happened the following days.

Christopher chose the clothes for J.C. to wear in the casket and what toys were to be in the casket. He gave J.C. his favorite toys, a coonskin hat, a stuffed Mickey Mouse and also some money for a bottle in heaven. Christopher was with his Mom and Dad and the entire family through the visitation time at the funeral home, the funeral, the burial, and afterwards as the families ate together and talked. Nothing was hidden from Christopher; therefore, I believe he was much more open with his questions, and his childlike faith had no trouble believing that J.C. was now with God.

The night after J.C. died was a clear, crisp March night and the stars filled the sky. Christopher looked up into the sky, found the brightest star and said, "That's J.C. watching over us."

And to this day on a clear night as I look up into the sky, I cannot but think that the brightest star in the sky is J.C. Without reservation, Christopher accepted the fact that J.C. was now in heaven, but he had questions about heaven. I believe a child's question should not go unanswered, and therefore, God gave to me a very special ministry for six months, to answer with love the questions of a five-year-old. Christopher asked these questions:

> Why did God take J.C.?
> Why did God take J.C. and not me?
> Why is J.C. special and I'm not?
> Why didn't J.C. take his body to heaven?
> Who killed J.C.?
> Who do you blame for J.C.'s death?
> What does J.C. eat in heaven?
> How did J.C. get to heaven?
> How far is heaven?
> What does God eat in heaven?
> How many calories does J.C.'s
> bottle have in heaven?

All these questions and many more needed to be answered in order to satisfy the mind of a five-year-old. No, there are no concrete answers since we do not know why certain things happen in the world and no one has been to heaven and come back to tell us what it is truly like.

For answers to these and many other difficult questions one must rely on the Bible and the common sense and faith given to us by God. We need to listen with our heart to the words God will give to us. These answers will help formulate the faith of one of God's children.

In regard to Christopher's questions, let me share with you a summary of the answers as I talked with Christopher.

"Christopher, God did not take J.C. It was an accident and now J.C. is with God. God did not kill J.C. but bad things like accidents happen in our world. J.C. was special in his own way and went to heaven. You are special in your way and are still here on earth for a purpose.

"J.C. is now in heaven. He does not need his earthly body because in heaven he received a heavenly body, a new body.

For what made J.C. and what makes you special is not just your body but your mind and personality, that is who you are, and your faith and love. Heaven is where God lives, and it is as close as our hearts and as far away as we can imagine because God is everywhere."

Christopher and I talked a lot about heaven and used our imaginations to think about what heaven would be like. The Bible gives us a picture of heaven to begin our thoughts and then we can go forward to imagine a perfect place of love, peace and joy with God. Since heaven is perfect, we decided J.C. would eat whatever was good and healthy for him and that God must be holding J.C. in his arms and giving J.C. his bottle. One day while at the cemetery, we talked about how far away heaven is. On J.C.'s grave marker is a baby angel on a cloud, and we thought maybe J.C. crawled to heaven on the clouds.

By using our imaginations while staying within the framework of scripture, Christopher and I were able to dream and talk about heaven as a very special place for J.C., and Christopher was very comfortable knowing his little brother was safe in the arms of God.

As I talked with Christopher, my own faith was strengthened as I received from God the reassurance that J.C. was in God's loving arms in a beautiful and wonderful place called heaven.

Children have so much to teach us if we will but listen. Listen to their questions and explore together the faith of a five-year-old.

**Prayer**

Father, we are Your children. May our faith remain childlike and simple. Thank You for the gift of children who remind us daily of Your love. Amen.

# Healing Begins At The Cemetery

**Scripture**
**Death is swallowed up in victory. O death, where is thy victory? O Death, where is thy sting? The sting of death is sin, and the power of sin is the law. But thanks be to God, who gives us the victory through our Lord Jesus Christ.**

- I Corinthians 15:54-57

**And Jesus said, "Where have you laid him?" They said to him, "Lord, come and see." Jesus wept.** - John 11:34-35

Fresh flowers in the flower vase, a six-year-old's drawing on the ground with a stone on top to hold it down, and I knew Tina had been here today as I stopped by the cemetery.

A mother's love never ends, not even at the grave. Tina is taking care of her son the only way she can now by keeping fresh flowers on his grave, bringing him little gifts for the season and taking care of the special flower bed made just for him.

Tina was devoted to her son while he was alive and is faithfully devoted to him now. Though she can no longer hold her son in her arms, she talks with him at the cemetery and cares for his little "bed of sod." Faithfully, she visits the cemetery making sure there are fresh flowers there at all times.

The cemetery is a place for the dead, but it is also a place for healing to come. As we come to the grave site of our loved one, we talk to him, tell him about what is going on in our lives, how much we miss him and how much we love him. Tears water the grass of the cemetery daily.

It is in these words, these prayers, these tears that healing comes. The reality that our loved one is gone begins to permeate our being, and we begin to awaken to the fact that our lives must go on though our loved one will remain here at the cemetery to remind us of his love, his life and all he taught us. The tears flow more easily at the cemetery, thus helping us to wash and cleanse our body of the emotions that we try to keep hidden within us.

It is in the quiet moments at the cemetery that we give ourselves permission to express the emotions we hold within us. It is here that tears, anger, and those unexpressed feelings are accepted, and we give ourselves the needed time to deal with the grief that we keep suppressed in our daily lives.

For some people the cemetery is a necessary step in the healing process; for others it may not be a needed continuous setting for healing. We all must face the cemetery sometime in our lives. It makes death a reality.

But there is hope in all of this. The cemetery is filled with earthly bodies, but God has promised when we enter heaven we will receive new bodies. Thus the hope and promise of death is that there is life beyond the cemetery. There is life in heaven with God.

Just as we cannot remain at the cemetery, neither can we live in the past wishing that our loved ones were still alive. We have to continue to live and to take what we have learned from our loved ones with us into our present and our future. Their love will always be with us in our hearts, and God will walk with us in our present; therefore, we are never alone.

**Prayer**

Heavenly Father, thank You for the gift of life and the promise and hope that when we die we are given a new life with You. Amen.

# An Angel Among Us

**Scripture**
**Behold, I send an angel before you, to guard you on the way and to bring you to the place which I have prepared.**

- Exodus 23:20

**And behold, an angel of the Lord appeared,... Now I am sure that the Lord has sent his angel....** - Acts 12:7,11

I believe in angels. I have always believed since I was a little girl that I have a guardian angel who watches over me and protects me. My angel has rescued me from troubles and near accidents many times.

I have also held an angel, not once but twice. Some may doubt they were angels because they looked like normal little boys, but God and I know they were angels.

As I stood in the chancel area of the church among friends for the baptism of Beau, a friend of the family, I cried tears of joy for the life of this six-month-old boy and the love that surrounded him this day. But I also cried tears of sadness remembering our own little grandson as I held him in my arms and baptized him two years ago.

Our grandson, J.C., is now an angel in heaven because at the age of 11 months he died. I truly held an angel of the Lord's the day I baptized J.C.

Since his death, my arms have ached to hold J.C. one more time because I never had the opportunity to hold him and to say good-bye. J.C. died while my husband, Dave, and I were on vacation, and by the time we arrived home, J.C. was already at the funeral home. J.C.'s parents and other grandparents held him at the hospital where he died and said their good-byes.

As the months passed, my need and longing to hold J.C. once more grew more and more intense though no one knew since I kept it all within my broken heart.

I prayed, "God, if I could just hold my angel once more and feel the warmth of his body, to see his smile, to touch his little hands."

And then Dave and I were invited to stand with the family at the baptism of little Beau. Dave had known Beau's mother since she was about as little as Beau. They are special friends of ours, and we felt honored to be present at such a wonderful moment as baptism. Beau was dedicated to God as all his family and friends promised to guide and support him as he grew in the faith and love of Christ.

After the service, there was a reception for Beau and his family at the church. It was a time of celebration and sharing together. Everyone wanted to hold Beau since this was the first time most had seen him since he and his family live in California.

Beau is a happy and very contented child who went willingly to anyone who wished to hold him. I hesitated in holding Beau since I was not a family member and there was so little time for family to be with him. But I walked up to the family member holding Beau and asked if I could hold him. Beau came to me immediately.

He snuggled up to my shoulder, smiled and laid his head down, and at that moment I knew God had answered my prayer. I was holding an angel, and for that short moment I was able to say goodbye to J.C. through Beau and hold him one last time.

A gentle peace and inner joy flowed through me. I held Beau close and kissed him on his forehead. He had given to me the most precious gift, and for a moment I thought I heard the brush of angels' wings above me.

While I missed our grandson, J.C., very much, I finally felt at peace that I had truly held him one last time through an angel named Beau.

**Prayer**

Lord, You know our inner needs. Thank You for meeting those needs gently with Your Spirit. Thank You for the gift of angels who watch over us. Amen.

Chapter 3

# Humble Servants
# Of God

*"Everybody has been so very kind helping me by calling and by their prayers."*

*— Grandma*

# The Greatest Man I've Ever Known

**Scripture**
**Whoever exalts himself will be humbled and whoever humbles himself will be exalted.** - Matthew 18:4

**Humble yourself before the Lord and he will exalt you.**
- James 4:10

**He who is lowly in spirit will obtain honor.** - Proverbs 29:23

One morning while listening to the radio, a song came on that described the greatest man ever known. I turned to my husband, Dave, and casually asked, "Who is the greatest man you've ever known?" This question then struck a cord deep within me and my mind raced through my memory and stopped at one special man. Dave, without hesitation, responded with that same special man, his brother, Don. We both laughed at how quickly but thoughtfully we had arrived at the same person, thinking that the other would name some world-renowned figure.

I asked Dave to qualify his choice, and we spent many wonderful moments talking about our greatest man, Don. Dave responded that even as a young boy, he always looked up to his older brother who was only four years older than he but mature beyond his years. Early in his life Don declared, not boastfully, but with conviction, that he was a Christian and Jesus was his Savior. Don had many great achievements, a wonderful marriage that produced two loving daughters, graduation from the United States Naval Academy at Annapolis. He earned his wings as a Naval aviator, became a surgeon, served tours of duty in Vietnam, and achieved the rank of Rear Admiral in the Navy.

Through all of these achievements, Don daily reads scripture and practices those things that give love, strength and encouragement to those with whom he comes into contact. He is always there in letter, via a telephone call or in person during the happy times and those times of tragic need in the loss of family members. Tears are not foreign to his cheeks. They are tears of strength, support and a deep love for those he comforts. Many people achieve great things, but Don's greatest achievement is the unselfish giving of his Christian love.

As a doctor, the term "bedside manner" has been given a positive step forward as he shares his love and compassion with his patients as if each were the most important person in the world. And at that moment the patient is the most important to Don.

My first encounter with Don was through a telephone call. I had never met Don but had heard wonderful stories about him through Dave as we shared our lives in our growing relationship. Don called me to send his love and congratulations when he found out Dave and I were going to be married. He talked with me as if he had known me forever and sent his love and prayers. His gentle spirit flowed across the telephone lines, and I already loved him as a brother before I met him.

As I have grown to love Don even more as my brother-in-law, I have developed the utmost respect and admiration for him. As I have learned about all of his accomplishments, achievements and travels, though he is very shy and humble to share them with you, I am in awe of all he has done with his life. But what makes him the "greatest man I have ever known" is his genuineness, his gentle spirit, his love and compassion. I have never known anyone with such deep, gentle and outward compassion, for when you are with Don, you become the focal point of all his gentle spirit and attention. Don makes you feel at ease and that you are the most special person at that moment. He lives his faith daily in all that he does in his work and in his home, naturally and without reservation sharing his love of Jesus Christ and his own need to depend upon Christ. When it comes to looking on the positive side of life Don walks the straight and narrow path, though he is always willing to take a stand on what is wrong.

I could describe in detail all the big and little things Don has done throughout his life which would be very uplifting, but being the humble man Don is, he would not want me to do it. But what I desire to convey in all of this is that being great is not based on human achievements or standards. Being great is what we do for God and for others gently and quietly without calling attention to ourselves; it is humbling ourselves before God. It is not based on possessions, wealth, popularity or power, but on the love and compassion of God which is in your heart that you give freely and unconditionally to others.

**Prayer**

Thank You Lord, for very special people in our lives in whom we see Christ and after whom we can model our lives. Teach us to humble ourselves before You, Lord, and serve You. Amen.

# The Lesson Of The Stones

**Scripture**
**Taking one of the stones of the place, Jacob put it under his head and lay down in that place to sleep.... So Jacob rose early in the morning, and he took the stone which he had put under his head and set it up for a pillar and poured oil on the top of it.** - Genesis 28:11,18

**Christ Jesus himself being the cornerstone.** - Ephesians 2:20

**The very stone which the builders rejected has become the head of the corner.** - Mark 12:10

When God created the earth, stones were included as a basic ingredient of the earth. God created stones to be used in the building of humanity's civilization. Jacob, when he fled into the wilderness, used a stone for a pillow and after his dream made an altar to God out of the common ordinary stones around him. The ordinary became holy.

Stones and stone quarries were central in the life of a special man named Kenny. As a teenager, he worked in stone quarries which began his life-long career and association with stone quarries around the state of Ohio. The highlight of many weekend trips with his wife and children was to visit a stone quarry.

Kenny's love of stones reveals his simple and basic understanding of life. Stone is a basic and simple part of life and is also a necessary ingredient for all foundations. Kenny lived a simple life and taught his family the basics and the foundation for life. He taught his children manners, always to say "Thank You" and "Please" and the importance of praying before each meal. Kenny was honest, spoke the truth and was genuine. What you saw was who he truly was inside. He taught his children not just in words but

53

in actions, always showing them how to do something, the basics.

Kenny's stones of love built a strong foundation for his family, a family that depended on each other and shared in each other's joys, accomplishments and sorrows. The foundation was built on faith in God, love of family and belief in what was good and honest.

As one looks at a stone from a stone quarry, it has rough edges and is not always pretty to the naked eye. Stones, though, when cleaned, shined and smoothed can be the most precious objects of beauty. Kenny did not have outward flare or beauty according to the world, but he shared himself very straight-forwardly and directly. He was just "plain old Kenny" with a heart of gold who was always there for his family.

In a stone quarry, one must dig deep to find the treasure of the stones. Within each person there is a treasure deep inside. "Man looks on the outward appearance, but the Lord looks on the heart" (I Samuel 16:7). We live in a world that judges people mainly on outward appearance, but what makes a person special is within the person. The important part of life is found within our hearts, and it is within our hearts that Christ wants to come and dwell to give us a forgiven and new heart.

We are called, like Jacob, to build our altars to God using the stones of our foundation of faith found within our hearts and from the experiences of our lives. Our altars become places of growth on our journey toward God. The events that are marked with altars may be times of deep sorrow or of joy, but always they are times of closeness with God just like the stones' closeness with the earth.

"Jesus said, 'I tell you, if these were silent, the very stones would cry out'" (Luke 19:40).

For Kenny, the stones did cry out with lessons for life. The stones taught him the basics of hard work, of building a strong foundation, and digging deep to find the true treasures of life.

Jesus is our Stone or our Rock. He is our Cornerstone of life. We are the stones which build upon the Rock of Jesus. We are to continue the building process, crying out about Jesus, sharing the love and joy of Christ, the basics of our foundation of faith and life with others. Listen to the lessons of the stones.

**Prayer**

Rock of God, guide me in building my life upon You, the Rock. Thank You for the simple gifts of life which teach me to depend upon You. Amen.

# Take Up The Mantle

**Scripture**
**Then he (Elisha) took the mantle of Elijah that had fallen from him,...** — 2 Kings 2:14

**For the Son of man also came not to be served but to serve, and to give his life as a ransom for many.** — Mark 10:45

**Greater love has no man than this that a man lay down his life for his friends.** — John 15:13

When you think of a modern day "servant of God" who comes to your mind? One may think about Mother Teresa, Albert Schweitzer or Billy Graham, all of whom are truly God's servants. Servants are people like you and me who give of themselves right where they live by sharing their faith, talents, gifts and love with those in need.

When I think about a servant, one special lady comes into clear focus, Teddy. Teddy was a member of the first church where I was a minister. Teddy married her high school sweetheart, Forest, and together they reared their children in a small town in Ohio. Teddy taught elementary children in Sunday School for over 30 years, even teaching the children of her former students.

Teddy had a very quiet and gentle spirit. She never raised her voice and earned the respect and admiration of children of all ages. After their children were grown and on their own, Teddy and Forest were inseparable, as Teddy helped with their propane gas business. Many times they would give the gas to needy families so their children would not freeze, and they could cook their meals. Teddy and Forest lived a quiet Christian life. Quiet in words and recognition, but busy in deeds and work. Their week included delivering meals to shut-ins, teaching a Bible Study to the elderly, volunteering in the church office, running errands for shut-ins, teaching Sunday School, securing the church building each night, and visiting the sick in the hospitals. Teddy was also a lay speaker and filled the pulpit many Sundays for area ministers. They helped begin the Chapel for Truckers. The list of their accomplishments is endless. Whatever they had, they shared with others. Their time and talent was given to God as well as their tithes and their total lives.

I could share with you story after story of famous men and women who have served Christ. To me, Teddy was a great servant. She was not famous outside of her small town nor did she travel around the world, but she served Christ right where she lived and thus gives each of us an example to follow. That is what makes servants great: they set good Christian examples for others to follow.

When Teddy died unexpectedly, Forest did not give up but took up the mantle of Christ that he and Teddy had carried together for years. He continues to serve Christ quietly and gently until God calls him home to be again with Teddy. Forest knows Teddy would want him to continue their work and he has done so in his own quiet, committed way.

Elisha took up the mantle of Elijah to carry on his work as a prophet after Elijah had gone up to heaven. When Christ died on the cross He gave to us His mantle, His work, to continue here on earth as His humble servants.

Being Christ's servant means using your talents and gifts right where you are. It is loving and giving to those around you and around the world where God is leading and calling you. Therefore, serving Christ is something within each one of us.

There is something each of us can do even if you are alone and your spouse was the strong leader of your family. Take up the mantle of Christ today and serve Him.

**Prayer**

Thank You, Father, for the example of Your Son, Jesus, who taught us what it means to be Your servant. May I serve You humbly where You have called me to be. Thank You for the example of Your servants among us that guide us in our daily walk with You. Amen.

# Worthy Of The Calling

**Scripture**
**I therefore,...beg you to lead a life worthy of the calling to which you have been called,...** - Ephesians 4:1

**And Jesus said to all, "If any man would come after me, let him deny himself and take up his cross daily and follow me. For whoever would save his life will lose it; and whoever loses his life for my sake, he will save it."** - Luke 9:23-24

My husband and I have a special friend who possessed a high calling in his job. Every time you saw President Bush on television whether in Washington, D.C., Maine, or Moscow, behind him or beside him you would have seen a tall, distinguished, dark-haired gentleman. This is our friend.

Our friend guarded the President of the United States. His eyes were always on the President and on the crowd. He was always alert and aware of those around him. His job was to keep the President safe, and he was willing at any moment to sacrifice his life for the sake of the man he guarded. He was called to go wherever the President went and keep the President free from harm or danger. Our friend had accepted the call of his profession and was truly worthy of his calling.

Our friend did not decide one day to protect the President. No, he developed his skills and knowledge and moved up the ladder in his profession, but there was much more to receiving this high calling. Knowledge and mechanical skills are necessary, but what is most important is what is inside the heart. Our friend is a Christian with a strong faith who knows God walks beside him. He is honest, above reproach and adheres to the highest morals and values. His standards are of the highest caliber and his integrity is beyond reproach. To receive and accept this calling one must be of this high quality.

59

You have been called to the highest calling, not to guard the President of the United States but the call of God to serve in the name of Jesus Christ. God calls you to grow in the faith He has given you and to adhere to the highest morals and values that God has given to this world.

God says that you are worthy. Do you believe it? I believe it. Will you accept the call of God in your life and be willing to go and do whatever God calls you to do? Are you willing to sacrifice for Christ as Christ sacrificed for you?

The call of God comes now to you.

**Prayer**

Heavenly Father, I believe that You have called me. Thank You for cleansing me in the blood of Jesus Christ and accepting me as Your worthy servant. Speak now, Lord, for Your servant is listening. Amen.

# Benny

**Scripture**
**And whoever gives to one of these little ones even a cup of cold water because he is a disciple, truly, I say to you, he shall not lose his reward.**                                    - Matthew 10:42

**And he who does not take his cross and follow me is not worthy of me. He who finds his life will lose it, and he who loses his life for my sake will find it.**                  - Matthew 10:38-39

Benny suffered through many surgeries and serious illnesses in his life. He had back surgery and heart surgery. He was then diagnosed with bladder cancer, went through chemotherapy and no trace of cancer was found in his system. Several years later Benny was diagnosed with lung cancer and went through chemotheraphy and radiation treatments. Complications set in and blood clots appeared. Benny's leg had to be amputated below the knee. Through it all, Benny was a real fighter. When you thought he would not make it this time, he rose above it and pulled through.

Benny made it through so much because he willingly laid down his life, and Christ carried him. Benny became an inspiration to many people. He kept his sense of humor through it all and told his infamous jokes. Benny was also blessed with a loving and devoted wife, Lois, who was always there for Benny in support and love.

Through the final years of his life, Benny still managed to go to the local drug store's old soda fountain where everybody knew him and talk with the local crowd.

Benny inspired these people not to give up because they saw his determination. Benny inspired many friends not to give up, encouraging others to do their very best. A week before Benny died, a group of Benny's friends, about 15 of them, gave up their

Saturday to build a shed for Benny's lawn equipment, mow, rake and fertilize his lawn. Why did they do all of this? It was out of their love for Benny. They willingly "laid down their lives" in a small way, as Benny had showed them how to do.

I will never be the same because of Benny. He called me his "angel" because I would appear at his home or in his hospital room just when he needed me. Through Benny's life, I learned what it means to lay down one's life so the Lord can pick you up and carry you. I learned that no matter what life gives to you, God gives you the strength and the fight not to give up if you but rely on Him.

The last thing I did for Benny was to hand him a cup of cold water as he lay in his hospital bed in his home. It was a simple gift of love, and I will always remember how Benny allowed me to give to him this simple gift in return for all he had given to me.

God works through the most simple gift of love to touch our hearts and lead us closer to Him. Because of Benny, I am more compassionate and willing to do the "little" things that mean so much to others.

The winds of life beat against Benny and eventually the winds of the Spirit took Benny home to be with God. The winds of life can beat us down and defeat us, but the good news is that Jesus comes to us in the midst of the storms and walks with us. We do not choose the storms, just as Benny did not choose his plight in life. But, like Benny, we can accept the storms and ride them with God as our anchor and our strength, never giving up for our trust is in the One who will steadfastly guide us through life.

**Prayer**

Thank You, Lord, for teaching me about the importance of the little gifts of life. Guide me in giving "cups of cold water" in Your name. As the storms of life beat around me and around those I love, may we all be anchored in Your love and strength. Amen.

# Ponder In Your Heart

**Scripture**
**Behold, I send my messenger before thy face, who shall prepare thy way; the voice of one crying in the wilderness: Prepare the way of the Lord, make his paths straight.** - Mark 1:2

**The time is fulfilled, and the kingdom of God is at hand; repent, and believe in the gospel.** - Mark 1:15

As I talked with a colleague in ministry and mentioned that I graduated from The Methodist Theological School (Methesco), he told me that Bogie had died yesterday. My heart immediately ached with sadness at such a great loss.

Van Bogard Dunn, or "Bogie" as everyone called him, was the founding Dean of The Methodist Theological School in Ohio and was also a professor of the New Testament with his specialty being the Gospel of Mark.

As a student at Methesco, I took two courses from Bogie, the Gospel of Mark and the Synoptic Gospels. Words cannot accurately describe the wonder of each course and the knowledge I gained from the mind of one who truly lived the Gospels.

To begin the class on the Gospel of Mark, the entire class gathered in the Chapel of the Seminary and listened as Bogie recited from memory the entire book of Mark. I had read the book of Mark many times, but for the first time I truly heard the Gospel as it was meant to be heard. I sat mesmerized as my mind went back in time and believed I was hearing the Gospel of Mark for the first time as it had originally been recited aloud.

I anticipated each class session, and class always ended too soon for me. I learned to read scripture with historical knowledge and present-day meaning, but most important, to read with my heart and hear the message of Christ. Bogie guided me in pondering scripture within my heart. Each class session would end with Bogie saying, "Now ponder these things in your little prune hearts."

I have many wonderful memories of Bogie: his smile that always made you smile, his wink, how he made you think for yourself, and how he would throw up his arms, smile when he saw me and give me a hug.

Bogie influenced me as a teacher who lived and believed what he taught. He was truly a messenger from God. Bogie was never satisfied with a class session or a seminar unless he was "provoked" in it. He would tell us if one was not provoked to action or change or challenged, it was not the Gospel being proclaimed. Bogie taught me much about life and the Gospel even though I would not consider myself a close friend. The Gospel needs to "provoke" me, to challenge me to go beyond myself and the limitations I place on the Gospel, and hear the Gospel as Christ intended it. The Gospel challenges us in our complacent way of thinking to live our lives as Christ lived. Are you provoked? Is your heart pondering the Gospel?

**Prayer**

Thank You, Lord, for teachers of the Gospel who challenge us and "provoke" us to living out the Gospel in our lives. Amen.

Chapter 4

# What God Hath Joined Together

*"You are one of my valentines. I know you will receive many from your friends and your family, it is a good way to let folks know they are loved. Even young couples can express their love this way. The first valentine I received from your Grandpa Clinger was when I was around sixteen years old."*

*—Grandma*

# Love Letters From God

**Scripture**
**I, Paul, write this greeting with my own hand. This is the mark in every letter of mine; it is the way I write.**
*- 2 Thessalonians 3:17*

**Beloved, if God so loved us, we also ought to love one another.**
*- I John 4:11*

"Dear .... How are you? I am fine." We have all written one sometime in our lives. We have all received one. A letter. When we open the mailbox and find one among the junk mail and bills, we are filled with anticipation and excitement to read the news from a friend or relative.

Some letters are filled with joy ... "We have a new baby." "Our daughter just graduated from college." "We bought a new home." Other letters express deep emotion ... "We express our sympathy on the loss...." "Dear John, I do not love you anymore..." "Dear Sweetheart, I love you...."

It began with a simple letter, "Dear Dave, My prayers are with you this weekend...." Then a Christmas card ...."Merry Christmas and Happy New Year." A note of sympathy followed several months later ...."You have been in my thoughts and prayers these past weeks and months...." Another letter... "Dear Dave, What a joy it was to hear that you were serving on this team...." Then came a phone call... "Can I see you?" A relationship had begun.

Now this was not just any relationship; this is how my husband, Dave, and I began our relationship of love. Dave and I met on the Walk to Emmaus Spiritual Renewal Weekend sponsored by the Upper Room of the United Methodist Church. I gave a talk on his weekend experience, and over the years we saw each other occasionally at The Walk to Emmaus functions and exchanged brief cards and notes.

It was a simple letter in which there was more emotion and feeling between the lines than the words written even understood. The words unwritten on paper but expressed unconsciously within began a relationship of love. God had brought us together through simple words on a piece of paper, or so we thought that they were simple. They were words that grew in emotion and depth from words seen by the eye, to words spoken on the telephone, to words spoken with a touch.

The first letter written was out of friendship and Christ's love expressing prayer and hope that God would renew Dave's love within his heart. The first telephone call, according to each of us, was fleeting hope; a desire from within that had no rhyme nor reason to become a reality. I was never home in the early evening, and Dave read my letter and "out of the blue" decided to call. To each of us nothing had been planned and it was mere luck, but in the eyes of God plans were now being carried out.

An everlasting relationship of love began with a word. "Can I see you?" "Yes." The heart wrote words of love before the mind knew there was to be a relationship. Our hearts were driven by the love of God who initiated our love.

Some may call it "magic" or "fate," but I call it the plan of God. I believe God brings people together if we will but listen to our hearts and truly follow the leading and voice of God.

Our relationship with God also begins with a word:

"In the beginning was the Word, and the Word was with God, and the Word was God." - John 1:1

God has sent us love letters through His Word, the Bible. God touches our hearts with his love coming to us in our inner soul and through words spoken in prayer. Finally we listen. God asks, "Can I see you?" God wants to have a personal relationship with each of His children. It is up to us to say "Yes" and accept the love relationship God offers us.

While Dave and I expressed our love in words through the letters we wrote while we were beginning our relationship, our love continues to grow and mature as we share our life together daily.

God not only gave us words of love, but He also came to earth out of love for us and lives with us daily.

"And the Word became flesh and dwelt among us, full of grace and truth...." John 1:14

**Prayer**

God, thank You for the gift of love that You love us and gave to us the greatest gift of love, Your Son, Jesus. Thank You that we can express our love to someone very special through the gift of marriage. Amen.

# What God Hath Joined Together

Scripture
**For this reason a man shall leave his father and mother and be joined to his wife, and the two shall become one flesh. What therefore God has joined together, let not man put asunder.**
- Matthew 19:5-6

**So faith, hope, love abide, these three; but the greatest of these is love.**                      - I Corinthians 13:13

On the first Sunday of 1990, the sun broke forth in full ray of hope and joy in the midst of the cold snowy winter in northwestern Ohio.  As the Associate Minister, I participated in two worship services as liturgist and shared with the children in the Children's Sermon.  This seemed like any ordinary, normal Sunday to be in the house of God, right?

This was not just the first Sunday of the new year, but the first day of a new life and beginning for me.  When the sun set on this Sunday, I would begin a new life as the wife of David Sturtz.

We chose to be married on a Sunday, on God's Day, to express to all persons our commitment to have Christ at the center of our marriage.  The entire church family of Celina St. Paul's United Methodist Church where I was serving as their Associate Minister, was invited to celebrate my time as their pastor and my new life as a wife, as I would move from this church family to begin my own family.

Dave and I wrote our own worship service. Yes, it was not just a wedding ceremony but a worship service where our family, friends and church family were participants in the service.  God's Spirit and love surrounded us in the 600 people who shared in our everlasting union.

The Worship Service began with this Call to Worship:

71

Pastor: Surely the presence of the Lord is in this place as we gather to celebrate the joining of two hearts in love.

Family: We acknowledge God's Lordship over our lives, and gather in God's presence to celebrate the uniting of Dave and Elaine, who were chosen by God to unite in this bond of marriage.

Pastor: God is love and has given to us the gift of love.

Family: It is with joy and gratitude that we share now in this service of love as Dave and Elaine come now to be made one in God and by God.

As the voices united in words of worship and song, my heart was filled with the deep and awesome presence of God and His great love. My heart overflowed with love for Dave, whom God had chosen just for me.

Dave and I shared the words we had written as vows of our everlasting love for one another:

"I commit my life totally unto you, here in the presence of God. I will always love you, need you and want to share my life with you. Together we will walk through this life as husband and wife, with God at the center of our marriage. I give to you now my faith, my life and my love."

As the wedding service concluded, I knew God was in the midst of our marriage and had joined us together forever within His eternal love.

A wedding is for a moment, but a marriage is for a life time. While our wedding was one of the high moments of my life, our marriage is the guiding light of each day, each moment of the rest of my life. I know that no marriage is perfect, but each day we work at our marriage, we love each other and tell each other that we do, we forgive one another, give to one another, and continue to grow and mature in God's love by keeping God at the center of our marriage. Dave and I are best friends who share the same values, goals and interests. We enjoy being with one another and feel incomplete when we are apart.

**Prayer**

Heavenly Father, thank You for the gift of marriage. May each of us who is married continue to strive and grow in our love for one another and love for You, keeping You at the center of our marriage. Amen.

# A House, A Home

**Scripture**
**The Lord will keep your going out and your coming in from this time forth and for evermore.**                    - Psalm 121:8

**Every one then who hears these words of mine and does them will be like a wise man who built his house upon the rock.**
                                                                - Matthew 7:24

**...no city or house divided against itself will stand...**
                                                                - Matthew 12:25

**... and I shall dwell in the house of the Lord forever.**
                                                                - Psalm 23:6

I heard the garage door close and watched out the window as he drove away into the cold January morning. The house was warm with heat, but my heart was cold and scared to be alone in this house for the first time. This was now my new home, but the memories that were here had nothing to do with me.

I slowly walked through the house as if looking at a stranger's home with nothing familiar around me. I touched a small figurine on a shelf and it seemed to ask, "What are you doing here?"

Dave and I had been married just two weeks, and those days were spent in the sun on our honeymoon. Now Dave had gone to work and I was alone in a house filled with eerie sounds that mocked my presence.

I walked silently through the house wondering what I would do today. Dave had told me to open drawers and doors and treat the house as my own, but the memories that lingered here seemed to forbid my entry. Each corner of the house, each object on the shelf had memories that were not mine but those of Dave's first wife and children who had lived here.

I walked upstairs and reverently walked into the room where she had died. Her warm presence I sensed, and I wondered if I could be the wife she was.

The first week I just walked all around the house, looking in drawers, opening doors, but then I felt like I was snooping, invading someone's privacy. The next weekend we packed up my "house" bringing back a few familiar items, though giving most of my possessions away since I would not need them. I brought back my Grandma's rocking chair and desk. I sat in her chair many times during the next months just to be near something familiar with my memories.

I prayed, cried, and tried to adjust to being a housewife. I loved Dave dearly and thanked God for bringing us together. I struggled with being a wife in "his" house.

We had talked about the house before we got married. If either of us was uncomfortable and could not live in the house, we would sell the house and move to a new house. But I knew Dave loved this house and to his children this was "home"; therefore I was determined to make this house our home.

I prayed each day and began to accomplish little changes and adjustments, but then I would touch a pan or towel and think, Iris used this," and those feelings of "why am I here?" would rush through me. I knew Dave's first wife, Iris, from the Walk to Emmaus Spiritual Renewal Weekend, and I had even eaten a meal in "their" home. I loved Iris as a dear friend, and knew in my heart she smiled down upon our marriage.

I believed that knowing Iris helped me to make this house our home. There had been love in this house, there was love here and there would always be love here. She was not my enemy or competition; she was my friend. Though early in our marriage, I had nightmares in which I had to share Dave, they eventually ended as Dave and I talked about his first marriage and the things he had learned that would make our marriage even stronger.

As time passed, we began to re-decorate, paint, new wallpaper, new furniture, and the house took on our personality as it became our home. It takes more than some re-decorating to make a house into a home. It was our love and commitment to God and to each other that has been the guiding force in making our house into our home.

Home is our place of refuge, comfort, warmth and security where we come to renew, refresh and re-create ourselves in our love. God is the center of our home and our lives. God wants to dwell in all of us, to be at home in us. "God is our refuge and strength, our present help in times of trouble." (Psalm 46:1) We all seek a home, and God, with His outstretched arms of love, waits to welcome each of us to be at home in Him.

**Prayer**

Thank You, Lord, for providing warmth and shelter physically and spiritually in our lives. Thank You for welcoming us home with You. Amen.

# The Magic Of Love

Scripture
**Love is patient and kind; love is not jealous or boastful; it is not arrogant or rude. Love does not insist on its own way; it is not irritable or resentful; it does not rejoice at wrong, but rejoices in the right. Love bears all things, believes all things, hopes all things, endures all things. Love never ends....**

- I Corinthians 13:4-8

**Let love be genuine....** - Romans 12:9

Today is our fourth wedding anniversary. Sometimes it seems like we were married just yesterday, and other times it is as if we have been together forever. Our love has matured into a deep and everlasting bond.

"I love you." Words spoken to one another each day since we first expressed the love in our hearts. There have been times when I have spoken these words and Dave has asked sincerely, "What is love to you?" The first time he asked, I felt a little insulted thinking he did not believe that I truly loved him. When my internal emotions quieted, I realized what a loving question to ponder.

We may say the words "I love you" without thought and without truly knowing what love is and why we love that special person. Love is a gift from God to each one of us. Because God first loved us, we can therefore love one another.

Well, "what is love to you?" My response to Dave was: "Love is caring, sharing my life totally with you, giving and forgiving, wanting to be with you." When Dave asked our grandson, Christopher, "What is love?" there was a slight pause and he responded, "It is closeness." I was impressed and thought that love is closeness, being together with the one you care for most deeply, close in touch and in spirit.

A recent movie talked about the "magic of love." When did you know it was love? For Dave, it was the first time he saw me after all our phone calls and letters. For me, it was the sound of his voice on the telephone. I knew then I would marry him and always love him. I believe the "magic" is the Spirit of God bringing together two hearts in love.

God touches our hearts with love so that we can love others and so we can love God. God loves us, forgives us and calls us to accept His love unconditionally and forever. The magic of love is found in the awesome love of God.

**Prayer**

O, God, I love You. Thank You for loving me and for giving the gift of love that I may love others. Amen.

# Trusting My Life To God

**Scripture**
**Trust in the Lord with all your heart and do not rely on your own insight. In all your ways acknowledge him, and he will make straight your path.**                    - Proverbs 3:5-6

As my thirtieth birthday approached, I felt that this was a milestone in my life. As a teenager and college student, the age of thirty was my goal for being where I wanted to be. At this age I believed I would have my career well under way and would be married with a family.

Now as I turned thirty, I began to look at my life. I was serving as an Associate Minister in the barren plains of northwestern Ohio, alone and no relationship in sight.

I had always prayed for God to bring the right man into my life, and now I began to believe that might never happen. About a month after I turned thirty, I felt a peace I had never felt before about being single. I began to accept the fact that I may serve in ministry all my life as a single clergy and that it would be O.K.

Once I accepted what I thought God had planned for my life, I was much more at ease with myself and my ministry. I enjoyed for the first time being single and the freedom that singleness gives to a person. I enjoyed my bike rides more, time with other families, and the peace and quiet of my home.

But then...God opened the door that I thought He had closed for my life. Why is it when you finally accept that this is what God has planned for your life and let go of what you want for your life, that God opens the door?

I believe when you release yourself totally to God, trust in God, and give every aspect of your life to Him, God will bless you with what you least expect but most need.

It was only three months later that God brought Dave into my life, and my dream at thirty changed dramatically. I was married to Dave at the age of thirty and took time off from ministry in the United Methodist Church to be in ministry within a family.

Is there something in your life that you need to release to God? Trust in God, and He will bless you. I know this is not easy, but it is necessary in order to live in peace and harmony with God's will and desire for your life.

**Prayer**

Lord, I give to You my life, all of my life. I trust in Your leading. Thank You, Lord. Amen.

Chapter 5

# The Faith
# Of Children

*"The children are a lively bunch, but they are very special to me as are all my great-grandchildren and grandchildren. The parents have a great responsibility in training them up so when they are older they will not depart from their faith in God."*

— *Grandma*

*"I know your faith will grow as you carry on His work."*

— *Grandma*

# I Shot The Lady

**Scripture**
**Truly, I say to  you, whoever does not receive the kingdom of**
**God like a child shall not enter it.**                - Mark 10:15

He was decked out in his brother's cowboy boots, a few sizes
too big, but that did not matter. They just made more noise on the
wooden floor as he dragged his feet. His gun belt was low on his
hip which made it easier to draw his guns. The cowboy hat was
down low on his forehead with the string drawn tightly under his
chin. His red bandanna was draped over his shoulder and tied
securely around his neck. He was ready for whatever awaited him
over the next hill, around the next corner or for that matter, in his
own basement.

The cowboy was not afraid to let everyone know he was coming by the sound of his boots clicking on the wooden floor. The
sound then grew faint and then a steady "Bang, bang, bang" ech-
oed down the valley as the cowboy rode down the hill of stairs.
He was afraid of no one, not even the strangers who rode into
town the night before and camped at the bottom of the hill of stairs.

He was brave and trusted in his fast draw to save him from any
danger. No one had seen him enter the strangers' camp. He did
not like people in  his territory. They had to be taught a lesson. He
jumped out from the bush of cabinets, quickly drew his gun and
shot the lady stranger.

He rode quickly back to his camp and proudly announced, "I
shot the lady."

This was my first encounter with Tyler. Tyler was the
four-year-old son of my husband's niece. We had come to
visit with them for a few days during a business trip. Tyler, in
his full cowboy attire, had greeted Dave and me early on our
first morning in their home with his guns ablazing as he "shot"

me and ran to tell his mother of his wonderful feat for the day.

In all the childlike courage Tyler could muster, and in the only way his childlike imagination could comprehend, Tyler had protected his home from the "strangers" who had entered. By putting on his cowboy outfit, Tyler became a real cowboy in his own mind and proudly "protected" his mother and family from the "evil" that awaited them at the bottom of the stairs.

Where is your childlike imagination? Did you discard it with your tinker toys and blocks? Do you think since you are an adult you can no longer dream and imagine great things? Listen to what Jesus is telling you: "Become like a child." Jesus does not want us to become stuffy, boring and only accept what we can see and only if we have all the facts.

Jesus wants us to trust, to have faith and believe in the things that are not seen. Jesus wants us to enjoy life with the childlike enthusiasm we once had; to use our imaginations and dream great dreams; to believe they will to come true with God's guidance and power.

**Prayer**

God, thank You for children who remind us that You call us to be childlike. Guide us as Your children to follow Your will for our lives. Amen.

# The Light Of Christ

**Scripture**
**You are the light of the world.**                    - Matthew 5:14

**Arise, shine; for your light has come, and the glory of the Lord
has risen upon you.**                                   - Isaiah 60:1

**God is light and in him is no darkness at all.**      - I John 1:5

The church was filled with the excited sounds of children whose
anticipation was difficult to suppress.  The smell of poinsettias
filled the air, and the light of the candles brightened the hearts of
all who looked deeply into the light with the wonderful excitement of Christmas.  The air outside was chilly with fresh snow
covering the ground in a blanket of white.  The feeling in the air
was breath-taking, and the church was filled with children of all
ages, waiting, waiting for Christmas.

It was Christmas Eve, and the Family Christmas Eve Worship
Service had begun.  The noise of the children "whispering" could
be heard throughout the sanctuary as children played excitedly
while parents tried with great difficulty to keep them quiet.

Then I asked the children to come forward for the Children's Sermon.  It looked as if I had opened the gates to a playground as children
ran forward from all the aisles to sit in the chancel area with me.

The chancel was filled with the beautiful white and red poinsettias and a large Advent wreath that rested upon a stand angled
down toward the people so all could see.  In the middle of the
wreath was the large white Christ candle about two feet high inside a two-foot candleholder.  The candles had been lighted earlier
in the service by one of the families in the church.  The candles
were shining brightly for all to see.

I had brought my Precious Moments Nativity scene to share

86

the Christmas story with the children. I began by asking what we needed to tell the Christmas story and as the children mentioned the characters for the story I added them to the scene: a stable, baby Jesus, Mary, Joseph, shepherds, sheep, wise men, camel, cow, angel, and a star.

As I laid out the entire Nativity scene, out of the corner of my eye I saw Joey. Joey was about three years old, and he had come that evening with his grandparents. Joey had walked behind me to get closer to the candles on the Advent wreath, and he began to blow out the candles one by one, slowly but deliberately. He walked around the large wreath and blew out the four outside candles. He leaned over the wreath to blow out the large white Christ candle, but he could not reach it. Joey started to climb over the wreath, but it was then that I stopped talking with the other children and said to Joey, "Joey, I'll blow out the candle for you."

Now the whole church family had been watching Joey as I had, and a hushed laughter pervaded throughout the sanctuary. I knew most of the adults were saying to themselves, "What is she going to do now?"

It was at that very moment that God whispered in my ear. I spoke to Joey and the children.

"Many times we, like Joey, blow out the light of Christ and do not allow Christ's light to shine at Christmas. We have the Christmas story before us through these figures, but what makes Christmas special is that Christ comes and gives us His light of hope and love. We are the light of Christ, and we need to shine in our dark world to tell others Jesus is born and Jesus loves you. We are what is missing from the Nativity scene, for we are the lights to spread the word of Jesus' birth and love. Let us be Christ's lights today and everyday."

When God whispers in our ear, we had better listen and be thankful. Thanks, God. God truly taught me a wonderful lesson through Joey.

We, as Christians, are the only lights Christ has in this world. Do we, like Joey, blow out Christ's light through our own selfishness or lack of faith or lack of willingness to share Christ with others?

Let your light shine for all to see not just once a year at Christmas but every day of the year. Be a beacon of light for others to find Christ.

**Prayer**

God, thank You for the gift of Your Son, Jesus, and for bringing light into this world of darkness. Guide me in being Your beacon of light that others may come to You through Your light in me. Amen.

# "Hello, Godmother"

**Scripture**
**Train up a child in the way he should go, and when he is old he will not depart from it.**                                        - Proverbs 22:6

"Hello, Godmother. You are my guardian angel," said the sweet innocent voice of my Godchild, Jennifer.

"That's right, Jenny, I am your Godmother, and I love you and watch over you," I replied.

Jennifer's mother, Peggy, had been talking with Jennifer, explaining that I was her Godmother, and she understood it to mean that I was her angel who watched over her.

Jennifer is four years old, and I was her live-in nanny for about five months of her early life. When Jennifer was baptized at five months old, her mother and father asked me to be her Godmother. I was honored to be given such a gift and a responsibility.

On the day of her baptism, I wrote this letter to Jennifer:

Dear Jennifer,

Today, April 15, 1989, you were baptized. It was a beautiful day filled with God's love, the love of your family, and the warmth of the sun. Today you outwardly became a part of God's family. God loved you even before you were born, and now your parents have outwardly expressed to the world that God loves you.

Baptism is your invitation into the family of God. Your parents have promised to rear you in a Christian home, to teach you the Scriptures, and to bring you to Church. They have promised to help you grow in God's love until you accept for yourself God's gift of love and grace through Jesus Christ.

I feel honored to be one of your Godparents. It is a privilege for me to assist your parents in your Christian growth and to be a positive influence upon your life. You are a very precious child. You will not remember our time together during your first five months on this earth, but I will remember this precious time and all you have taught me through your unconditional love. God's love is also unconditional; God will always love you no matter what you do or where you are. You will always be loved.

Jennifer, you have a family that loves you very much. Your grandparents and most of your aunts and uncles and cousins shared in your special day. Your great-grandmother was here to share in your baptismal celebration and you talked with her and smiled in your special way bringing joy to her life. God has given you a gift already to bring sunshine and joy into people's lives. Always believe in yourself and share the gifts and talents God has given to you.

You are a precious and special child of God.

Your Godmother

What does it mean to be a Godparent? I promised before God to assist my friend, Peggy, and her husband, Don, in teaching Jennifer about God. This is an awesome responsibility that is not just ceremonial. Jennifer now sees me as her "Guardian God-mother Angel," and I want to be God's human vessel that will assist in bringing Jennifer closer to God. Parents need help in rearing their children in this secular world. Children need positive Christian influences in their lives in addition to their parents.

God has called each one of us to care for His innocent children. "Hello, my Godmother, will you watch over me?"

**Prayer**

God, You love us as Your very own children. You have given us the awesome responsibility of caring for Your children. May we be good and wise examples for children to follow to You. Amen.

# A Love Note

**Scripture**
**So we know and believe the love God has for us. God is love, and he who abides in love abides in God, and God abides in him.**                                                    - I John 4:16

The envelope read "I love you" in the top left corner where the return address usually is written.  In the middle of the envelope were these words, "From Rachel" with "Rachel" being underlined five times.  Next to her name she had drawn a flower; it looked like a tulip to me.  I opened the letter.

The letter was folded the way a seven-year-old would fold it, just so it would fit into the envelope.  I unfolded the paper.  At the top in large letters was written, "I LOVE YOU."  A two-story house with three windows (curtains drawn in each window) and one door was drawn in the center of the letter.  On one side of the house was a little girl with the word "Me" over her head.  On the other side of the house was a woman with the word "You" written over her head.

This letter was written by my niece, Rachel, when she was just seven years old.  It resides among my "precious treasures."  In these "treasures" are cards, pictures and letters that have deep sentimental value.  They are irreplaceable keepsakes that I will read at special moments in my life and cherish for years to come.

I am sure you have some "precious treasures" tucked away in a box on a shelf in the back of your closet, in a drawer, or even in your purse or desk.  Maybe they are artwork or school papers from your children or grandchildren, a love letter from your spouse, or a special card from a dear friend.  You take them out when the mood is right, read them, cry over them, laugh with them.  They may be torn and wrinkled, tear-stained and smudged, but they are more precious than gold.

I have shared some of my special letters with you, written by my Grandmother and my husband. Why is Rachel's so special? Rachel is a special niece just as each of my nieces and nephews is special in his or her own way. Rachel, though, reminds me of myself when I was her age. There is even a physical resemblance, but there is much more.

Her words express simply, but most profoundly, her desire to be loved and her love for me. She wants to be with me, just the two of us together. I remember having that desire and need as a child, too. Children need visible signs and expressions of love.

We each long to be loved. A child's innocent letter reminds me that God loves me and wants us to be together, just the two of us in a love relationship. God loves you. He wants you to accept His gift of love, and then He wants you to share His love with one another.

**Prayer**

God, You love me! Thank You for always loving me. There are so many people who feel unloved and unwanted. Use me as Your vessel of love. Amen.

# Found By God

**Scripture**
**It was fitting to make merry and be glad, for this your brother was dead, and is alive; he was lost, and is found.** - Luke 15:32

**For the Son of man came to seek and to save the lost.**
- Luke 19:10

**I love those who love me, and those who seek me diligently find me.** - Proverbs 8:17

**O Lord, thou hast searched me and known me!** - Psalm 139:1

We are a seeking people. We search for ways to make our lives easier, search for happiness, for wealth, for understanding, for love, and for meaning to our lives. We all search in some way for God, seeking ways to draw closer to God. What we need to realize is that God is a seeking God. God tries to reveal Himself to us, but He remains hidden from us because we are not looking for Him in the everyday happenings of our day-to-day lives. Down deep inside each of us there is a longing, a desire to be found by God.

A group of youth was playing the game "sardines" during an overnighter at the church. Sardines is a form of hide and seek; one person hides and the rest of the group try to find the one hiding and then hide with the person until all persons are in the hiding place.

One of the youth to hide was Meggan, who was a petite eleven-year-old. She found the perfect place to hide, a rarely-used closet behind some old hanging choir robes. Meggan sat on a small ledge in the back of the closet and put her feet up so no one could glance into the closet and see her. And it worked. The group looked for

93

a long, long time, up the stairs, in the closets, through the kitchen. No one could find Meggan. Some of the youth wanted to give up and call the game off, but we could not find Meggan to tell her.

Meggan was so excited that she had hidden so well no one could find her secret hiding place. But then it occurred to her, "They are not going to find me." Then Meggan began making noises whenever someone walked by the closet in which she was hiding. And soon they all found her. And Meggan said, "Oh, you found me." What Meggan really wanted was to be found.

What you and I really want is to be found by God and to find God. It may seem like God is hidden or far away at times. God wants us to find Him, and God comes many times when we least expect Him. We find God only when we stop long enough to listen to the still small voice of God that calls to us within our hearts. Our search for God may be long and demanding, but in the end it is worth it.

**Prayer**

Lord, I want to be found by You. Keep me open to Your leading and do not let me shut the door of my heart to You. Lord, I once was lost but now am found. Thank You. Amen.

# Following An Example

**Scripture**
**For to this you have been called, because Christ also suffered for you, leaving you an example, that you should follow in his steps.**                                          - 1 Peter 2:21

**So that you became an example to all the believers....**
                                                    - 1 Thessalonians 1:7

**For I have given you an example, that you also should do as I have done to you.**                         - John 13:15

"Let's play follow the leader. I am the leader. Let's go." And out the classroom, down the hall and out the door we went as the children followed me into the bright sun of a cloudless Sunday morning.

We have all played the game "follow the leader" sometime in our childhood, but do we still play the game as adults? Whose example are you following?

As an aunt with 15 nieces and nephews, I have been aware most of my life that these young people look up to me and watch what I do and what I say. They believe if Elaine does it, it is right to do. My mom used to say, "If you went to the moon, they would follow you."

When I was a student at Otterbein College, my niece, Jodi, was in kindergarten. She accompanied my mom one Friday afternoon to pick me up at college and come home for the weekend. Jodi was very impressed with the whole college scene, and told us on the drive home that she would be going to Otterbein College following the example of her aunt.

Now I was very proud of Jodi, that she would want to attend such a fine school as Otterbein when she graduated from high school. But Jodi said she was going to go to college now. I laughed and said, "You have to go to first grade next, not college."

"O.K.," said this smart six-year-old, "I'll go to first grade and then I'll go to college."

It took most of the trip home to explain to Jodi that she had to attend school for twelve years and graduate from high school before she could become a college student. Jodi wanted to be doing what I was doing. And in her little six-year-old mind, she thought if it was good enough for her aunt, it was good enough for her.

Whose example are you following? I am sure, like me, you have had many good examples in your life, your parents, grandparents, aunts, uncles and teachers. Each person had special gifts and qualities that you admired which you have tried to incorporate into your own life.

We each have the greatest example to follow for our lives, Jesus Christ. God became man and dwelt among us so that we would have an example to follow. God wants us to follow Christ in how we live our lives.

As Christians we are examples of Christ for others to follow. How is your life reflecting Christ? There are people right now who are being guided in their lives by the way you live. Be a good Christian example for others.

**Prayer**

Lord, it is an awesome responsibility to be Your example in this world. Guide me daily to follow Your Word, to talk with You and to live my life as You would have me to live. Amen.

# God In My Heart

**Scripture**
**If you confess with your lips that Jesus is Lord and believe in your heart that God raised him from the dead, you will be saved.** - Romans 10:9

**And let the peace of Christ rule in your hearts, to which indeed you were called in the one body.** - Colossians 3:15

**Now faith is the assurance of things hoped for, the conviction of things not seen.** - Hebrews 11:1

"How does God get inside my heart?" a little boy asked me in Junior Church after I had talked during the Children's Sermon about God living in our hearts.

"We ask God to come in our hearts and be a part of our lives," I replied.

And then the rest of the children joined in with questions;

"I thought God was in Heaven, so how can he be inside of me?"

"I don't feel God inside of me."

"How can God breathe if he's in my heart?"

"How can God get that small to be in my heart?"

"If God is in my heart, how can He be in yours, too?"

How do you explain this abstract concept to little children? For that matter, how many adults really comprehend how God can live within our hearts, be in the world, be in Heaven and be with each person in the world?

That's what faith is all about. Believing what we cannot understand or comprehend because God says it is true.

As I talked with the children about their questions, God whispered into my ear again. First of all, I talked about love. "Who do you love?" They loved their parents, their brothers and sisters, their grandparents and their friends. "How do you know you love them? Do you feel love in your heart for them?" "Yes."

"God is more than a feeling in your heart, but that is part of it. Right now you are not with your parents, but you know where they are because you just left them in the sanctuary. Think about your parents. Imagine them being with you right now. They are not actually here in this room, but they are with you in your thoughts. God is with you in your thoughts, but there is more to God than just thinking about Him."

"Now think about the last time you were with your best friend. Being with your friend is special. You probably talked with your friend and shared something with him/her you would not share with anyone else. God is your best friend with whom you can share anything. He always listens and is always with you."

"God is a feeling, a thought, a friend and much more."

The children accepted this on faith, believing God was in their hearts because they felt Him, thought about God and knew He was their friend.

As we mature, we seem to lose some of our childlike faith, and we want concrete answers to all our questions about God. God is an awesome God whom we cannot fully comprehend because we are human. If we understood all there was to know about God, then God would not be God. That is the mystery, and that is where faith comes in. We accept God into our hearts and lives and accept on faith those things we cannot fully comprehend because God asks us to accept.

**Prayer**

God, I cannot comprehend the vastness of Your being, but I do believe and know You live within my heart. May I accept You and Your love with childlike faith. Amen.

# Two Hearts

**Scripture**
**Create in me a clean heart, O God, and put a new and right spirit within me.** - Psalm 51:10

**Blessed are the pure in heart, for they shall see God.**
- Matthew 5:8

**For where your treasure is, there will your heart be also.**
- Matthew 6:21

With thirty-five cents "burning a hole" in his pocket, Christopher and I headed for a short trip to the grocery store. Next to the grocery store was a small Christian bookstore. Driving past the store I remembered that I needed to find a small praying hands to use in an upcoming talk. Christopher was, to say the least, reluctant to go to the bookstore because he wanted to spend his money in the gum ball machines at the grocery store. With his "pouty" look on his face, he followed me into the store.

Christopher immediately found the toys in the store, examining each to see if it was worthy of his money. After being told countless times that he did not have enough money to purchase an item, Christopher found a small pocket cross with a card explaining the cross. It fit his budget, and he purchased the cross.

After we arrived home, Christopher pulled out the cross from his pocket and asked me to read the card to him. The card told the significance of the cross, Christ died on the cross and the cross is therefore the symbol for a Christian.

Christopher asked, "What is a Christian?" Then for the next few minutes I shared about Christ with a five-year-old. I asked Christopher what happened at Christmas.

"Jesus was born," he replied.

"Then what happened at Easter?"

"Jesus came to life," responded Christopher.

"That's right. On Good Friday, Jesus died on a cross. He died because He loves us and died for our sins. Sins are the things we do wrong. Being a Christian is when you ask Jesus to come into your heart and you live for Jesus."

Christopher said, "Oh," accepting the words I had just shared with him, but his little mind was still thinking.

Several minutes later Christopher did something wrong. He was sitting on a chair at the table as I tried to explain to him that what he had done was wrong and that I wanted him to be a good boy. Christopher looked straight at me and said, "Will you train me to be good?"

My heart smiled with joy at his innocence and sincerity, and as I hugged him I responded that that was what I was trying to do.

Later that day, after I had read several books to Christopher as was our nap time tradition, and before he lay down to sleep, Christopher, who I could tell had been in deep thought, said to me, "I wish I had two hearts, then I would be really good."

Two hearts. Yes, if we had two hearts we would be really good. But we do not need two hearts, just a forgiven heart. Through Christ's death on the cross, we have been forgiven, and given a clean and new heart. And as we follow Christ as our example, He "trains" us to be good.

Do you need a new heart? Ask Christ to come into your heart, to forgive you and cleanse your heart, and He will train you to be "good," to be His disciple.

**Prayer**

Lord, Jesus, come into my heart. Forgive me, cleanse me, renew me. Give to me a clean heart. Amen.

# A Gift From The Heart

**Scripture**
... and a little child shall lead them.                    - Isaiah 11:6

For the wages of sin is death, but the free gift of God is eternal
life in Christ Jesus our Lord.                    - Romans 6:23

But earnestly desire the higher gifts.          - I Corinthians 12:31

So I thought it necessary to urge the brethren to go on to you
before me, and arrange in advance for this gift you have promised, so that it may be ready not as an exaction but as a willing
gift.                                               - 2 Corinthians 9:5

O'Shay, Christopher and I journeyed to the grocery store one
spring day as we shared the day together. The store was having an
anniversary celebration and was giving balloons to each of the
children. Naturally, O'Shay and Christopher were eager to receive their free gifts.

On the way home from the store, Christopher's balloon burst,
and he wanted O'Shay to burst his balloon. But O'Shay held on to
his balloon and said, "I'm going to give my balloon to J.C."

My eyes immediately filled with tears as O'Shay thought of
his cousin who had recently died wanting to give him a special
gift to share in the day.

"How can you give it to J.C.?" Christopher wanted to know.

"Wait until we get home," I told both of them.

We pulled into the garage, and the boys jumped out with O'Shay
holding tightly to his helium-filled balloon.

"Where is J.C.?" I asked our two little grandsons.

"In heaven," they replied in unison.

"Where is heaven?"

"Up there." They both pointed to the sky.

At that moment O'Shay released his balloon into the air, and we watched it float gently up into the sky, and then it caught a wind current that swept it out of our sight.

"How long do you think it will take to reach J.C.?" asked O'Shay.

"He already has seen it and knows what a wonderful gift you have given him," I said as I hugged O'Shay.

The unselfish gift of a child. O'Shay willingly and unselfishly gave a small but priceless gift to the cousin he loved. His childlike faith believed J.C. would receive the gift in heaven.

Children know that the simple gifts are the best. They scribble on a piece of paper with a crayon and give it to us in love. It is priceless. But soon we adults teach them that the cost of the gift is more important, through commercials and store advertisements which entice children into this material outlook, and thus the beautiful, childlike quality of simplicity disappears.

As we mature in years we find joy and contentment in the simple things of life again, a sunset, the painting of a child, a hug, a note of kindness, a phone call just to say "hi."

O'Shay also expressed a sincere and simple faith. He believed his cousin was in heaven and that earth could touch heaven through the gift of a balloon. And I believe it did.

Jesus calls us to come to Him as children and believe, but we try to make faith so complicated and want to come to God on our own terms. That is not possible. It is a free gift given to us only by God. It is simple, maybe too simple for our complicated world. God made it simple so everyone could come to Him, even a child.

Heaven touched earth through God's gift of His Son, Jesus, and it is through Jesus that we know and accept God. All we need to do is come to Christ with a simple childlike faith and say "Yes" to Him and He will come into our hearts to live forever.

**Prayer**

Heavenly Father, I come to You as Your child. I accept Your free gift simply into my heart. Forgive me when I try to complicate Your gift of faith. Amen.

# My Master

**Scripture**
**A disciple is not above his teacher, nor a servant above his master, it is enough for the disciple to be like his teacher, and the servant like his master.** - Matthew 10:24-25

**Neither be called masters, for you have one master, the Christ.**
- Matthew 23:10

**And Jesus said, "You call me Teacher and Lord; and you are right, for so I am."** - John 13:13

Our grandson, O'Shay, has been taking karate lessons, Tang Soo Do, from a Korean Master Kim. O'Shay has progressed from a white belt, to a yellow belt and now has passed the test to receive his orange belt.

One day as Dave and I were talking with O'Shay about his lessons, he told us his teacher was Master Kim and when he talks with you in class you must respond to him by calling him "Sir." Dave asked O'Shay, "Why don't you call me 'sir?'"

And without hesitation, O'Shay replied, "Because you are not my master."

Tang Soo Do is teaching O'Shay discipline, respect and coordination along with a skill of self defense. It is through an excellent "Master" that O'Shay is learning this skill.

After watching one of O'Shay's tests, Dave and I could see what an excellent "Master" and teacher Master Kim is. All the young children listen intently to Master Kim and he has no discipline problems in his class. What is his secret, I wondered? He was teaching these young children a skill but in order to accomplish the skill he taught them discipline and respect as a part of the skill.

We have all had wonderful teachers somewhere in our lives whether in school, Sunday School, or a relative or friend. We looked up to them, respected them and believed in them because of who they were and how they cared for us. We followed their advice and worked harder for them because in them we saw traits we admired and wanted to be like them.

Who is your master or teacher now? Whom do you respect, admire and follow each day of your life? We have one Teacher, one Master who calls to us to follow Him, to listen to Him, and to trust and believe in Him, Jesus.

## Prayer

Master, there are so many voices calling for my attention and allegiance, but may I listen only to Your voice and follow You as the Master of my life. Amen.

Chapter 6

# Growing As
# A Christian

*"I am thankful you are serving in church work as a disciple of the Lord. We all need to grow in the Christian faith, so we can help and share our faith."*

*— Grandma*

*"You have entered into college with high aims and been very active, which is very good, so be careful as you plan your future. Forgive me if I have written too much, but that is what I have experienced in life, to know and follow God's teachings in the Bible the best I know how."*

*— Grandma*

# What Do You Want To Be?

**Scripture**
**I press on toward the goal for the prize of the upward call of God in Christ Jesus.**                         - Philippians 3:14

"What do you want to be when you grow up?"

When I was five years old, my parents bought our first television set. My parents allowed me to watch the children's show "Romper Room" while my brothers and sister were in school. One day there appeared on the show the funniest yet strangest person I had ever seen. It was a clown. He had on the biggest bow tie, and he kept tripping over his huge shoes. He had what looked like a little ball on the end of his nose and hair that stuck out all over. I began to laugh as he tried to juggle. And I knew what I wanted to be when I grew up.

Then I went to school. My first grade teacher, Mrs. Hughes, was so loving and kind. She understood when I cried and allowed my sister to visit me to help me adjust to school. She really cared about me and made me feel so special. She even chose me to sing in the Christmas pageant. And I knew what I wanted to be when I grew up.

When I was about nine years old, my grandmother took me to the Wyandot County Museum in Upper Sandusky. My hometown was the last settlement of the Wyandot Indians in Ohio, therefore the museum was filled with Indian artifacts. I went home that day and began digging in our garden looking for Indian arrowheads. I was positive one of the rocks I found was  used by the Indians. And I knew what I wanted to be when I grew up.

Then during the summer before attending eighth grade I went to church camp for the second year at Camp Wesley in Bellefontaine. This time I went without friends or anyone from my home church. At first I was scared, but I soon made new friends and had a wonderful time. The last night of camp, we had a commitment service on Vesper Hill. Each person was given a twig from the surrounding trees, and we were told if we wanted to accept Christ into our lives to come forward and place our twig on the altar. I came forward and committed my life to Jesus Christ. And I knew what I wanted to be when I grew up.

I had a goal for my life as a junior high youth, and I was pressing on to be the best Christian in the world. But I could not understand why I kept making mistakes and why I was not yet perfect. Unfortunately, I believed I could achieve being a Christian by works and by being good. I kept goofing up, and it seemed I could not achieve my goal.

Then I went to church camp the summer after my senior year in high school, and I completely surrendered my life to Christ. I asked for forgiveness and began to understand that one does not become perfect when one accepts Christ. One continues to grow and mature and "press on" toward the goal. It was at this church camp that I accepted God's call into the ministry. And now I knew what God wanted me to be and to become.

Through my ministry I have fulfilled my childhood dreams. I have become a Christian clown, witnessing for Christ through clown ministry. I have become a teacher, teaching children, youth and adults about the love and grace of Jesus Christ. I have found a greater treasure than mere arrowheads; I have found the treasure that will not rust or decay, the treasure of Heaven.

"Press on" toward the goal to which God calls you. God wants us to be all He created us to be. It does not matter what your age, do you know what God wants you to be when you grow up?

**Prayer**

God, You have created me as Your special child. Guide me in becoming all You created me to be. Amen.

# The Voice

**Scripture**
**And after the fire a still small voice.**                    - I Kings 19:12

**And God said, "...."**                                        - Genesis 1:3

The telephone rings. You wonder, "Who is calling me?" You answer and a smile crosses your face as you hear, "Hi, it's me." A familiar voice.

We hear voices every day from the radio, the television, on the phone, at work, at school and on the streets. Some of the voices are familiar, some we hear but do not listen to what is spoken, and some voices are just noises we tune out.

Do you know someone who has a distinctive voice, a voice you could pick out of a crowd, a voice that is so distinctive that no one could imitate it?

My cousin, Lucille, had one of those voices. It was a nasal kind of voice that was crisp and clear and always gentle and kind. I never heard her say a harsh word. The gentleness of her voice made you feel welcome in her home, and as she talked you felt her spirit of love flow from her heart to her words and touch you.

The last time I heard Lucille's voice it was weak but still clear and gentle as she lay in a hospital bed as cancer was slowly taking her body, but not her spirit. Her words always encouraged me and filled me with love, for she and her husband regarded me not just as a "cousin" but as one of their own.

I can no longer hear her voice since she has gone to be with our Heavenly Father, but if I close my eyes and concentrate, I can still hear the voice of Lucille saying, "Now LeRoy," which was her favorite saying to her husband, LeRoy.

Can you hear a distinctive voice today? It is a voice amidst the noises and crowds of daily living, or have you tuned this voice out as just another noise? You know the voice to which I am referring. Yes, it is a voice like no other voice that comes to us in the midst of our busy lives, but it seems so hard to hear.

The voice becomes clearer and more distinct in the quiet moments of our lives as we pause to reflect, to seek guidance and to pray. When we come to a quiet place to rest, it is in this solitude that the voice whispers in our ear.

Yes, this is the voice of God.

The voice of God comes to us when we are quiet enough, patient enough and willing truly to listen. God calls to each one of us, and we need to be polite enough to listen. The voice of God comes to each one of us differently, but it comes to all of us if we will but listen with our hearts.

What is God saying to you today? Are you listening?

**Prayer**

Speak to me, O Lord, for I am listening. Amen.

# Listen To Me

**Scripture**
**And I heard the voice of the Lord saying, "Whom shall I send, and who will go for us?" Then I said, "Here am I! Send me."**
- Isaiah 6:8

**Hear my cry O God, listen to my prayer;** - Psalm 61:1

**And the Lord came and stood forth, calling as at other times, "Samuel! Samuel!" And Samuel said, "Speak, for thy servant hears."** - I Samuel 3:10

"Please do not interrupt while I am talking."

"But I want you to listen to me."

Words spoken by a mother and daughter, but these words could also be spoken between God and His children. God calls to us, but sometimes we are talking too much even to hear God. Listening is as much a part of prayer as talking.

During the summer after I graduated from high school, I was feeding the sheep late one night. It was always my job to do the chores at night. I had fed the lambs grain and went out beside the barn to the water pump and began to fill my five-gallon bucket with water to carry to the lambs inside the barn. I had carried several buckets of water and paused to rest a moment.

I looked up into the sky and saw thousands of brilliant stars and a full moon staring down at me. At that moment I felt the presence of Someone with me. I looked around and there was no one. I knew the Presence I felt was the very awesome Presence of God. A magnificent peace and assurance filled me that night. You see, I had just answered God's call into the ministry at a church camp a few weeks earlier, but I still wondered, was it really the call of God or just my wish to be called? Listening to God sometimes is just being quiet and knowing God is with us giving us His reassuring presence.

But that night, out beside the barn, looking up into the starlit sky, I felt God's personal presence with me as I had never felt it before. I heard God speaking within me, "Yes, I am here with you, and I will always be with you. I have chosen and called you. Listen to me."

How do you know God has called to you? God calls each of us to our professions to do His work, to minister to other persons throughout the moments of our lives. You may not hear an audible voice from heaven, and therefore at times are unsure where God wants you to serve and unsure of what God wants you to do.

I believe God calls us in many different ways. Remember the story of Elijah who had gone into the cave out of fear of being found by those who wanted to kill him. A great wind, then an earthquake and fire came to Elijah, but God was not in any of them. Then came a still small voice. Sometimes God speaks loudly, but most of the time God comes in the still small voice within us. We just need to listen.

My husband, Dave, has a special saying, "Listen to me, trust me, follow me and I will get you there and I will get you back."

I believe God says to us when He calls us -

"Listen to me and I will speak to you.
"Trust me when you are afraid and unsure.
"Follow me for I will guide you.
"I will get you to your calling in life.
"And I will bring you back home to Me."

If we will listen to God as God speaks through other people, events, the Bible, situations and within our hearts, I believe God will call each one of us to serve Him and to live our lives for Christ.

**Prayer**

Speak, Lord, for Your servant is listening. Amen.

# A Special Place

**Scripture**
**And after Jesus had dismissed the crowds, he went up on the**
**mountain by himself to pray. When evening came, he was there**
**alone,**                                          - Matthew 14:23

**Thou art a hiding place for me, thou preservest me from**
**trouble; thou dost encompass me with deliverance.** - Psalm 32:7

**For he will hide me in his shelter in the day of trouble; he will**
**conceal me under the cover of his tent, he will set me high**
**upon a rock.**                                          - Psalm 27:5

**And in the morning, a great while before day, he (Jesus) rose**
**and went out to a lonely place, and there he prayed.**
                                          - Mark 1:35

I saw it in the distance as I climbed the wooden gate next to the barn, my haven from work. There at the end of the field was our woods. Oh, it was not a huge forest; it was not even a small woods, just two rows of trees with a ditch in front of them, about 25 trees in all, but it was my grove of trees.

I grew up on a small farm with cows, sheep, pigs, chickens, dogs and cats. My dad also planted crops of corn, beans, wheat and oats along with hay to bale for the animals. My dad had a strong work ethic in which he believed work always came first. Sometimes it was difficult for me to accept that I had to finish all my chores before I could play and relax.

The woods became my haven of rest and play for a short time between all the chores. My brother and I had built a rustic tree house in the corner tree. Most of the trees were pine trees, so I would gather pine cones and pretend they were food for frontiersmen who were traveling through on their way westward. Or I would make a trail with the pine cones for Hansel and Gretel to follow. Other times I would sit in a tree and listen to the birds sing or the wind blow through the trees. I'd listen really closely and think I could hear the voice of God whisper through the trees. There was so much to do and to imagine in my little woods. Then in the distance, I would hear the voice of my dad calling for me. Oh, I did not want to leave my special place, but I knew I had to. But I also knew I would be back again.

I still have a favorite place where I go to be alone and to listen to and talk with God. It is my grandmother's rocking chair in our bedroom. I call it my prayer chair. It is where I pray most of the time. When the day is difficult, problems arise, decisions need to be made or I need to rest from my work, I sit in Grandma's chair. I talk with God, but mainly I just listen as I look at Grandma's picture beside me. And like the woods, I know I cannot stay in my chair and let the world pass me by, but I know, too, that I will be back soon, very soon.

We all need a special place where we can go and just be alone, just listen to life and calm ourselves and find peace. We need a place to be alone with God and where God has our total attention away from the noise and hustle of the world, our work and our worries. Jesus knew the importance of being alone with God and His need to talk with His Father. So do you. Answer that longing within you, and find a special place to be alone with your thoughts and God.

**Prayer**

Heavenly Father, thank You for always being with us and Your willingness to listen and talk with us. May I always take time for You and to quiet myself to listen to You whisper in my ear. Amen.

# Chosen

**Scripture**

**You did not choose me, but I chose you and appointed you that you should go and bear fruit and that your fruit should abide,**
- John 15:16

**For you are a people holy to the Lord your God; the Lord your God has chosen you to be a people for his own possession, out of all the peoples that are on the face of the earth.**
- Deuteronomy 7:6

**Do you see him whom the Lord has chosen? There is none like him among all the people.**
- I Samuel 10:24

**...even as he chose us in him before the foundation of the world, that we should be holy and blameless before him.**
- Ephesians 1:4

**God chose you from the beginning to be saved, through sanctification by the Spirit and belief in the truth.**
- 2 Thessalonians 2:13

I had been chosen. I was excited. Mrs. Hughes, my first grade teacher, had chosen me along with five of my friends to be in a special singing group for the school Christmas play to represent all the first graders.

We were all dressed as animals to be given as gifts to the girl who was the main character in the Christmas play. I was chosen to be a tiger, and my mom made my tiger suit. The suit was made from tiger print material, had a long, stuffed tail and a cap that went over my head with ears just like a real tiger. We sang our song, and though I do not remember any of the words to the song,

116

I do remember how excited I was. Someone took a picture of our little animal group which I still have to this day.

This was my first performance. I must have done well, because I was chosen each year to be in a special singing group for the annual Christmas play at my elementary school.

What a wonderful feeling to be chosen. It makes you feel special, set apart, gifted. Some people allow this feeling of being chosen to be a negative expression when their ego and selfish pride take over and they believe they are better than anyone else. These people then look down upon other people who were not chosen and regard themselves as a better class of people. How sad.

No, the feeling of being chosen to which I am referring is a very positive expression. The best way of being chosen does not depend on your beauty, your voice, or your athletic ability. No, the best way to be chosen is to be chosen by God. And each of us is chosen by God. We are special and set apart by God to do His work in this world. God has chosen each one of us for a special task, for a special work and reason.

Throughout the Bible God chose people, God chose Abraham to be the Father of a great nation, He chose Moses to lead the Israelite people out of bondage, He chose David to be the King of Israel. God chose the prophets, the judges, and Jesus chose His twelve disciples. All of these people were chosen by God, set apart for a special task. These people were not perfect nor better than their peers. Some, like Moses, wanted God to choose someone else, for Moses said he was not "eloquent in speech."

The Bible tells us that these people were chosen because God believed in them and they were faithful and responded to the call of God. God chooses you, and it is your responsibility to accept the call and to accept being chosen by God.

**Prayer**

Thank You, Lord, for choosing me. I accept the responsibility of being one of Your chosen people. Open my heart to listen to what You call me to do and to be as Your chosen one. Amen.

# In The Shadow Of Thy Wings

**Scripture**
**Be merciful to me, O God, be merciful to me, for in thee my soul takes refuge; in the shadow of thy wings I will take refuge, till the storms of destruction pass by.** - Psalm 57:1

**For thou hast been a stronghold to the poor, a stronghold to the needy in his distress, a shelter from the storm and a shade from the heat...** - Isaiah 25:4

"A thunderstorm will pass through our area sometime in the night," was the weatherman's prediction. As I turned off the radio, I knew it was going to be a good night for me to sleep. I usually sleep so peacefully through storms.

Many little children and adults are scared of storms. The loud thunder and the bright lightning brings fear into their hearts. Hiding under a bed becomes the common behavior during a storm for children and even a few adults.

As a child, I loved thunderstorms. I still love to watch the lightning and see the miracle of God in the storm. Though I know and have experienced the destruction of storms, they are still a part of the miracle of creation.

One of the reasons that I am not scared of storms is that as a child whenever there was a storm, especially at night, my mom and brother, Bruce, would get up and watch the storm. Bruce was fascinated with changes in the weather and used to predict the weather accurately, to my amazement.

They would stand by the window and watch the direction of the storm. If it was tornado season, they would watch the cloud formation, and if there was a sign of a tornado they would wake the rest of the family to head to the basement until the storm passed by. Once, though, I remember watching a tornado go over our house but not cause any destruction. Knowing, though, that my mom and brother were watching the storm and if we needed to go to the basement, they would wake me, I usually slept right through the worst storms. I knew I was being watched over and had nothing to fear.

I still sleep the best through storms, having no fear or anxiety about them. I know I am being watched over even though my Mom and brother are not with me. I know God is watching over me. God never sleeps and never leaves us in the storm alone. God watches over us as we sleep.

We all encounter storms in our personal lives, too. Are we filled with fear, or do we have the assurance we are being protected and watched over by God? God is our refuge and strength through the troubled times of our lives. If we will but turn to God, He will walk us through the storms. That's right, God walks through the storms with us, not always around the storm. We have the comfort of knowing God is always with us no matter what happens in our lives.

**Prayer**

God, You are my refuge and strength. Hold me close through the storms of life and never let go of my hand. Amen.

# Forgiveness

**Scripture**
**If we confess our sins, he is faithful and just, and will forgive our sins and cleanse us from all unrighteousness.** - 1 John 1:9

**For I will forgive their iniquity, and I will remember their sin no more.** - Jeremiah 31:34

**And forgive us our debts, as we also have forgiven our debtors.** - Matthew 6:12

**...forbearing one another and, if one has a complaint against another, forgiving each other; as the Lord has forgiven you, so you also must forgive.** - Colossians 3:13

"God, it is time I finally forgive myself and let go of the past so I can take up life in the present. I keep beating myself down with what I have done wrong in the past. So many times I have given it to You for Your forgiveness. I know You have forgiven me, but I keep taking it back and will not forgive myself. God, it is time I quit feeling sorry for myself, and accept Your forgiveness and the fact that I am not perfect nor will I ever be perfect. But I do not have to be perfect for You to love me and to use me as Your servant. God, I have believed that I had to uphold a certain image for others, and therefore, I tried to hide the things I had done wrong out of fear that if they found out they would not like me anymore. God, help me to believe in people, and though they may be disappointed in what I have done, they will not quit being my true friends. Help me to forgive and to forget so that I can live in the present as Your forgiven child."

Forgiveness. Jesus died on the cross so that we may be forgiven. God has made forgiveness easy for all of us. All

God asks us to do is come to Him, confess our sins and ask for His forgiveness. God will forgive our sins and remember them no more. All we have to do is accept His forgiveness. Easy? No, it is not easy because we make it hard for ourselves.

We would rather God tell us we had to do something to earn the forgiveness instead of it being a free gift of God's grace. God forgives us, and then He forgets our sin. Human beings tend never to forget the sin even if they have been forgiven. When we dwell on the sin, we are saying God has not forgiven and we call God a liar.

Healing can come to our lives only when we accept God's total forgiveness and when we forgive others and forgive ourselves. Sometimes it is difficult to forgive ourselves, thinking we are not worthy of God's forgiveness. The truth is, we are not worthy. We will never be good enough, smart enough or perfect enough to be worthy of God's forgiveness. No one deserves God's forgiveness. It is a free gift of love which God gives to all persons who will accept it.

Whom do you need to forgive? Is there something inside you that needs to be forgiven? Do you need to forgive yourself? Begin now. Seek and accept the forgiveness God offers.

**Prayer**

God, forgive me for my sins. Help me to forgive myself and to get on with my life. Amen.

# The Least Afraid To Risk

**Scripture**
**Not that I have already obtained this or am already perfect; but I press on to make it my own, because Christ Jesus has made me his own.**                    - Philippians 3:12

**Yet, O Lord, thou art our Father; we are the clay, and thou art the potter; we are all the work of thy hand.**          - Isaiah 64:8

God, I have always been afraid to fail, and therefore, I have been unwilling to risk. I fear failure because I have lived in a perfection mode, and if I failed I would no longer be perfect. God, I have never been nor will I ever be perfect. I have thought if I do not try something I can still maintain the illusion of being perfect and intelligent, but if I try and fail then my imperfection will be exposed.

God, help me to be willing to risk, and if I fail, help me to admit my failure, but may it not defeat me so that I do not keep trying new things for You. I need to admit my mistakes and when I do something wrong, I need to admit it instead of trying to make an excuse or blame someone else.

God, I have always felt inferior and thus have been afraid to try new things and to risk. God, I have known what it is like to be "least." For I felt like the least in school. My family did not have personal wealth, I was not pretty, nor was I popular with my peers. I was just average in my eyes, and that was not good enough. I tried to compensate through academics, but there was always someone who was better. I realize now that I was allowing the world's standards and other people to give me my identity and to help me feel good about myself when it was my responsibility. I denied Your truth that You created me as special and did not believe in my own uniqueness.

God, if I am to grow, I must be challenged. Help me not to run away from challenges of life but to face them with You as my guide and strength.

God, I am Your child, and I am not inferior to anyone else. With You in my heart, I can have the confidence to attempt anything You ask of me. God, You have called me to be faithful to You, not successful in the eyes of the world. Amen.

Are you willing to risk the only life you know which is unfulfilling for the life God wants you to live? Are you willing to venture out in faith, trust in God's leading and become all that God created you to be? Go for it!!!!

**Prayer**

Hear, Thou my prayer, O, Lord. Amen.

Chapter 7

# Attitude Toward Life

*"Some folks say 'you look pretty well,' I say I am thankful for that much."*

*— Grandma*

*"I always try to do something extra each day, keeps me more active."*

*— Grandma*

*"Your mother said you were getting over the shingles. Your head is a very necessary part of your body so take care of it. HA! My head gives me troubles too."  (I had shingles in my hair and on my face at the time.)*

*— Grandma*

# The Wait

**Scripture**
**But they who wait for the Lord shall renew their strength....**
- Isaiah 40:31

**Put on then as God's chosen ones...patience....** - Colossians 3:12

**But the fruit of the Spirit is...patience....** - Galatians 5:22

**Be still before the Lord and wait patiently for Him.**
- Psalm 37:7

One thing my dad taught me was patience. Now I did not learn patience through Dad's example but on having always to wait for him. I determined a long time ago that I could either become angry and allow Dad's constant tardiness to affect my life bitterly or I could relax and believe God was teaching me patience the hard way. I opted for the latter, knowing it would build strong character and less stress and ulcers.

Dad was never in a hurry to go anywhere until it was time to be there. For the first 18 years of my life, I can count on one hand how many times we arrived at church on time even though we lived only a few miles away. Dad even taught my siblings and me patience on Christmas. Our home was heated with two wood-burning stoves. Dad would purchase the outside bark of logs which was thrown away at the lumber mill and use it for firewood. This wood had to be cut or "buzzed" on our buzz saw which was hooked up to our tractor flywheel by a large belt. Dad always seemed to think we needed more wood on Christmas morning and invariably we had to "buzz" wood before we could open our presents. Waiting and anticipating was a natural part of Christmas in the Clinger household.

Dad also loved to shop in hardware and tractor supply stores. Now it does not take me long to go into one of these stores, find the part or supply I need, pay for it and be out the door. But not my dad. He could spend literally hours in one store looking at each bolt, nail, bucket or food supplement for animals. I believe I have literally spent at least one full week, 168 hours, of my life in these stores waiting for my dad. Out of boredom, I learned all the different types of nails, screws and hand tools. No amount of whining or complaining would hurry up Dad. He would be ready to leave when he was ready.

At the time I encountered these tests of my patience with Dad, I was not anxious to learn patience. Patience is not looked upon as a virtue by an adolescent. But as I now reflect upon these experiences, I am grateful to Dad for this invaluable lesson of patience which has been an asset to my life.

Patience is a necessity of life, and Paul regards patience as one of the fruits of the Spirit (Galatians 5:22). We need patience in driving our cars, in our work, with our families, and especially in our relationship with God.

God does not work on our time schedule, for God's timing is uniquely different than ours. When we pray we expect an immediate response from God but that rarely occurs. God teaches us to wait and have patience as we trust in Him.

**Prayer**

Heavenly Father, patience is sometimes difficult for me as I live in a fast-paced world. Quiet my mind and spirit to wait patiently upon You. Give me patience with my friends, family and people I meet each day. Amen.

# Garbage Cookies

**Scripture**
**Since all have sinned and fall short of the glory of God.**
- Romans 3:23

**A cheerful heart is a good medicine, but a downcast spirit dries up the bones.** - Proverbs 17:22

Filled with frustration, I dumped all my freshly baked sugar cut-out cookies in the garbage. They were dry and covered with flour. I had added too much flour to the recipe because the batter had been too sticky. I had not read the recipe carefully before starting and now realized these were drop cookies not cut out cookies. I wanted to make Halloween cookies for our new neighbors and our son's neighbor, but now they were in the garbage.

I raked leaves today and filled the pumpkin trash bag with the leaves and set the pumpkin under the tree for decoration. As I finished my task and the grass was vacuumed of leaves, the wind began to blow and took hold of the leaves still clinging to the branches and brought them gently down to where I had just raked.

I went to the grocery store for just a couple of items, but forgot to check on my basic staples and ran out of flour, sugar and brown sugar and had to return to the store before I could finish my baking.

My day had been very frustrating. I could have very easily taken it out on my husband when he arrived home, but he would not understand and would be an innocent recipient of frustration and anger. I could be angry at myself and thus ruin a good evening with my husband. I could eat to appease my frustration or do nothing for the rest of the day but sulk and feel sorry for myself. But instead, I stood quietly in my kitchen and prayed to God:

"God, you know how frustrated I am over these "little" and insignificant things. Forgive me, and help me to see the humor in all of this and give to you my misplaced anger and frustration. Release me from these feelings about things that will not matter tomorrow so that I can live more joyfully today. Amen."

Yes, a little prayer sent to God at the right time helps a lot. It calmed me down enough to see that what happened was not devastating, and it would not matter tomorrow. Yes, I made some mistakes, but my prayer gave me a different perspective on my daily events.

Not everything we do turns out perfect. We all make mistakes. Let's just face them, admit them, ask for forgiveness if needed, and go on and learn from them. I learned to check my recipes more closely for what I really want to make and to check my supplies before going to the grocery store.

And about leaves, well, I'm glad I raked them so I could fill my pumpkin bag and when I looked at what the wind had downed, well, it was beautiful to watch the leaves ride the wind and scatter across the yard. If the wind keeps blowing, maybe all our leaves will blow next door and then into the woods so I will not have to rake them!

It all depends on our attitude and perspective toward life. Many times we give "little" things too much power and importance. We need to ask ourselves, "Will this matter tomorrow, next week or next year? What difference will it make in my life or the world?" We can let little things really "bug" us and affect our relationships and our attitudes, or we can laugh at them and learn from them. It is all up to us. God is always there to listen to our prayers in the midst of our "garbage cookies."

**Prayer**

Thank You, God, that You are always with me and You care about the little frustrations of my life. Amen.

# Power Of Words

**Scripture**
**Keep your tongue from evil, and your lips from speaking deceit.**                                    - Psalm 34:13

**Your tongue is like a sharp razor....**                    - Psalm 52:2

**A soft answer turns away wrath, but a harsh word stirs up anger.**                                    - Proverbs 15:1

**Let the words of my mouth and the meditation of my heart be acceptable in thy sight, O Lord, my rock and my redeemer.**
                                                        - Psalm 19:14

Ever have one of those days when everything you said was received by others as negative and not what you really meant to say? Have your words become jumbled and mixed up from your brain to your tongue? Have the words you have spoken changed someone's attitude though you never intended for it to happen?

Words! They can bring comfort and joy in times of sorrow and loneliness. Words can express the deep love you have for another. But words can also hurt, bring hatred and a change in attitude.

Words have power not just in what is spoken but in how they are spoken and how they are received by another. Your attitude, facial expressions, and body language play a vital part in your words.

Today, every time I spoke to my husband, Dave, without meaning to bring anger or a change in his attitude, I did. There was no reason for these words to bring sadness, misunderstanding and distance between us but they did. I said, "I'm sorry," but each time I have spoken today it has changed his attitude. He said he heard something in the way I spoke that was negative and demanding though it was not intentional on my part.

What can I do or say now? How can words bring healing today? I have been quiet for awhile now. I have cried to release my feelings of anger and frustration. I have prayed not so much in words because I do not trust my words right now, but in feelings and through my breath. I have breathed in God's Spirit and breathed out my feelings of anger, resentment and confusion.

After being apart for awhile, we each said, "I'm sorry," kissed and made up. We later talked about our words, and accepted that it was our attitudes inside more than the words that caused the problem. The important thing was that we did not let this problem continue, but we were able to communicate our feelings and to help each other work through the problem.

Each day of our lives we talk to people. Our attitudes, whether negative or positive, will affect those with whom we are in contact. How's your attitude? Is God and His love reflected in your words? Are you communicating a good attitude?

Communication is essential, but lack of communication dries up relationships and closes doors. We need to talk with one another to grow in our friendships. We need to talk with God to grow in our relationship with God. Communication involves talking, words and listening.

**Prayer**

God, my attitude sometimes gets in the way of my words. Forgive me. Help me to keep the lines of communication open with my loved ones and especially with You. Amen.

# Obstacles To Grace

**Scripture**
**I do not understand my own actions. For I do not do what I want, but I do the very thing I hate.** - Romans 7:15

**Jesus himself bore our sins in his body on the tree, that we might die to sin and live to righteousness. By his wounds you have been healed.** - I Peter 2:24

**I acknowledged my sin to thee, and I did not hide my iniquity; I said, "I will confess my transgressions to the Lord"; then thou didst forgive the guilt of my sin.** - Psalm 32:5

On one visit to my parents when I lived in Marysville, I left Marysville and headed north on Route 4 and turned onto Route 37 driving through some small towns. As I curved through one town, Essex, I saw the dreaded sign, "Detour 14 Miles Ahead." I had forgotten all about this detour, never thinking it would still be here, but it did not bother me since the last time I just went around the detour on some familiar country roads.

I continued driving and as I neared the small town of LaRue, I saw the roadblock in front of me. A different bridge was out, and I had just passed the last intersection. So I had to back up my car, turn around and go down some unfamiliar country roads, around the detour and then back onto the main road, going an extra three miles. "That was easy enough," I told myself. "No problem getting to my parents' home now."

Little did I know that as I entered the small town of Marseilles another bridge was out, and I could not even get out of Marseilles my usual way. Again, I had to back up my car, turn around and detour around the town on some back roads. Now these were very familiar roads, roads I had traveled on in a school bus as an elementary student. So I thought, "No problem, I will just take the 'scenic route.'"

Then I turned onto the road where my home church is located. I came to the last crossroad on the road where there is a small hill. As I came over the hill, I saw that the road was flooded. I hit my brakes and made a quick turn to the right at the crossroad. As I drove down this road, I came to some mud across the road and then some high water about a foot deep even though there had been no "High Water" sign at the intersection. I drove through the high water and rounded a curve and found mud about a foot deep across the road with high water beyond it. Again, I had to back up my car, turn around and go back through the foot of high water and go an extra five miles around the high water to finally reach my parents' home.

What a trip! What began as a simple and routine trip became a trip filled with roadblocks, detours and obstacles. I thought I would never make it, but I finally reached my goal.

Roadblocks and obstacles seem to get in the way of where we want to go in life, too. Our lives are filled with many obstacles which get in the way of our closeness with God and our acceptance of God's loving relationship.

What do you do when you encounter a roadblock or obstacle? Do you just stand there not knowing what to do? Do you retreat to safety, never to venture out again on the road? Or do you figure a way to get through or around the obstacle to reach your goal?

God wants to walk with us through these obstacles and help us to overcome the burden of them, the burden of our sin. God gives to us His love and forgiveness through the gift of His Son, Jesus Christ, who died on the cross for our sins. What is your greatest obstacle in life?

What is preventing you from being all God created you to be and to live in close fellowship with Christ? Name your obstacle before God, and God will help you to begin at once to obey Him in the first thing you can think of in which you are not obeying Him. Begin now.

**Prayer**

God, thank You for being with me through the obstacles of my
life. I name before You my greatest obstacle. Forgive me, and
help me to begin now in overcoming my obstacle and being obe-
dient to Your will. Amen.

# The Big Rock

**Scripture**
**And I tell you, you are Peter, and on this rock I will build my church, and the powers of death shall not prevail against it.**
- Matthew 16:18

**He only is my rock and my salvation, my fortress; I shall not be greatly moved.** - Psalm 62:2

**The Lord is my rock, and my fortress, and my deliverer, my God, my rock, in whom I take refuge, my shield, and the horn of my salvation, my stronghold.** - Psalm 18:2

The Big Rock was at the end of the playground under a large old tree that had shaded the Rock for many years. The Rock was smooth to the touch from years of children sitting upon it, touching it with their dirty hands, and even from a few tears shed upon it.

The Big Rock was on the playground of my elementary school. The teachers tried to keep the children away from it. They said it was too close to the road, but they really did not want to walk that far to check on the children at recess.

The Rock was a place to go to have a quiet talk with a friend, and the rest of your classmates would know not to go there while you talked. It was also base in a game of tag.

The more "popular" kids tried to control who could be at the Rock. Being in control of the Rock gave one power and popularity. Being included at the Rock meant you were accepted by the crowd.

The Rock itself never changed over the years except for becoming smoother. It always accepted everyone who came to sit upon it. The Rock was very simple and never pretentious. It had no favorites and never objected to being sat upon, though teachers seemed to frown upon it. The Rock, for my friends and me, was a place of safety and security. It was a place to think, reflect and to share your feelings and thoughts with a friend.

We all have a "Big Rock" in our lives, a Rock of safety and security. The Rock is always with us, is steady and sure, and has become smooth from years of being sat upon and used. The Rock is where we go to reflect upon our lives and to share our feelings.

Our Rock is God Himself. God calls us to come to Him and sit under the shade of the old tree and talk with Him. God is always there willing to listen, to accept our tears, and to smooth out our lives. Just come to the Rock.

**Prayer**

Lord, You are our Rock and our Salvation. You never change. You are steady and sure. May we always rely on You and come to You who will listen to our hearts. Amen.

# Before The Lamp Goes Out

**Scripture**
**Again Jesus spoke to them, saying "I am the light of the world; he who follows me will not walk in darkness, but will have the light of life."** - John 8:12

**The lamp of God had not yet gone out....** - I Samuel 3:3

**You are the light of the world. Let your light so shine before men, that they may see your good works and give glory to your Father who is in heaven.** - Matthew 5: 14, 16

When I was in the eighth grade, English was not my favorite subject. My English teacher did not help my attitude when she gave us the assignment to memorize a poem. The longer the poem, the more extra credit, and I needed all the extra credit I could get in English. So I chose to memorize a very long poem.

I began reading and re-reading the poem days before the assignment was due. Finally I had to get serious about memorizing the poem. The night before the assignment was due, I set aside the entire evening for memorization. That night a storm blew in and knocked out our electricity. My mom had to cook supper on our old wood stove, and I had to read by candlelight. So beside my candle, I struggled to memorize my poem. I can still hear Mom say, "You better hurry up and get your homework done before the candle goes out."

The next day in English class, I told my teacher about our electricity going out and how I had to study by candlelight, but I still had to recite my poem. As I began, my friends seemed to listen sympathetically knowing it was a struggle for me the night before to do my homework, and it was a struggle for me to remember the poem. The class encouraged me when I forgot and applauded when I completed the poem.

This incident is very vivid in my mind. It would have been just another assignment had not the electricity gone out. I would have failed the assignment if my candle had gone out. And because of the unusual circumstances my classmates listened and responded with affirmation because of my determination which strengthened my self-assurance.

Many times the lamp of hope and determination goes out in our day-to-day lives. We seem to live in darkness and do not see any light at the end of the tunnel. No one is there to encourage us to keep trying and not to give up. We do not know how to rekindle the fire and light the lamp of hope.

But Jesus comes to us and says, "I am the light of the world." Jesus comes to light our way when all we see is darkness. If we will but call on Him, Jesus will come and light the path for us to follow giving us hope, guidance and assurance that we are not alone.

**Prayer**

Heavenly Father, You are the light of the world. You gave the world light and bring light into the darkness of my life. Thank You. Amen.

# The Lawn Chairs

**Scripture**
**Trust in the Lord, and do good...**                    - Psalm 37:3

**Trust in the Lord with all your heart and do not rely on your own insight.**                    - Proverbs 3:5

**Finally, brethren, whatever is true, whatever is honorable, whatever is just, whatever is pure, whatever is lovely, whatever is gracious, if there is any excellence, if there is anything worthy of praise, think about these things.**    - Philippians 4:8

They lined the main street of town early in the week for the big Homecoming Parade. Some were tied together with ordinary string, but most were just laid along the curb side in anticipation of the big parade. They were lawn chairs of every size, shape, color and material stretching over six blocks of the main street of town. No one touched or disturbed the chairs. Every chair remained where placed by the owner until the parade. No one stole the chairs or destroyed any of them as a prank.

No, this is not a story from 30 years ago, but what happens each Homecoming in the town of Celina. People trust one another. Homecoming is the greatest celebration for this town, and the people respect its tradition and importance. No one moves or destroys another person's lawn chair, and each person is allowed to choose his/her spot to sit and watch the parade. Usually people choose the same place year after year, and it becomes "sacred ground" to them. The United Methodists usually gather on their "sacred" lawn and have a Methodist get-together on Main Street.

The parade occurs on a Saturday evening and lasts over two hours. It is not so much what is in the parade that is so important, but that the people have gathered as a community to show support to the parade participants and to have fellowship with their friends and neighbors.

A simple lawn chair can teach us much about life. It reminds us about the importance of the simple things of life and the simple values and morals  handed down from generation to generation from God. Our society sometimes muddies the water for us when it comes to values and the simplicity of life.

A lawn chair left by the curb reminds us of the importance of personal property and its sacredness. It is very difficult to trust in our world of crime, selfishness and hatred. But there is one whom we can always trust, God. God never fails us, never leaves us and it is in God we can put our ultimate trust.

I know there is evil all around us and our society's values and standards are not in keeping with God's. But if we dwell in the negative, we will allow fear to take hold of our lives and isolate and immobilize us. There is good in the world. Look at the lawn chair. Look for the good in the simple things. What simple thing do you see today that can teach you about life and trust?

**Prayer**

Lord, in Thee I put my trust. Guide me to see the good in the simple things of life today. Amen.

# Snow Shovel Theology

**Scripture**
**Submit yourselves therefore to God.**                    - James 4:7

**So whatever you wish that men would do to you, do so to them;**
                                                    - Matthew 7:12

**We who are strong ought to bear with the failings of the weak, and not to please ourselves; let each of us please his neighbor for his good, to edify him.**                    - Romans 15:1-2

From time to time, there are days when each of us does not feel well physically or mentally though we are not really sick enough to stay home.  On these days you just want to curl up with your favorite blanket and not move for the rest of the day.

But have you ever noticed that on these days when you do get out of bed though you would have rather slept the day away, when you do something for someone else you do not even notice or feel the pain or sickness?

It had snowed about ten inches, and I had shoveled our driveway.  The next day our neighbor's mother who was housesitting while her daughter and son-in-law were in Florida was attempting to shovel their driveway.  Now I knew she was not a well person and had had heart problems in the past.  It was bitterly cold out, and she had no business shoveling snow.

I put on my hat, coat and gloves and grabbed our snow shovel and shoveled her driveway.  I sent her into the house to rest and get warm.  The whole time I was working, I did not feel the pain and sickness I had felt when I got up in the morning.

After I finished and went home, the feelings of sickness came back.  I wondered why.  Then I thought, when we do something for others our focus is no longer on ourselves and our little pains, but on what we can do to help someone else. God gives us the extra strength to help someone in need.

That morning during my prayer time, I had prayed that God would guide me to help someone that day. And God did. All day I felt better that I had listened to God's nudging and did not focus on my little aches and pains.

It is so easy to get caught up in ourselves and to excuse ourselves from reaching out to others because of a bad back, cramps, or being too tired. When we get the focus off ourselves and onto God, God will lead us in doing His will and work. We need to be open to His leading and nudging to do the little and simple things for others that mean so much. That's right, the little things mean so much to people for whom we would take the time to help and care.

What is God calling you to do today? Find your snow shovel.

## Prayer

God, keep nudging me. Don't let me make up excuses which You know are not true anyway. Nudge me today to help one of Your children. Amen.

Chapter 8

# Ministry Of Sacred Moments

*"You are receiving training like Timothy did from St. Paul."*

— *Grandma*

*"I hope and pray this last year of Seminary will establish you more firmly in your faith and capability as a minister of the Gospel."*

— *Grandma*

# The Sheep Of His Pasture

**Scripture**
**The Lord is my Shepherd....**                              - Psalm 23:1

**Behold I, myself will search for my sheep, and will seek them out.**                              - Ezekiel 34:11

**I will seek the lost (sheep), and I will bring back the strayed.**
                              - Ezekiel 34:16

**"I am the good Shepherd. The good Shepherd lays down his life for the sheep."**                              - John 10:11

I grew up on a small grain and animal farm on which my dad raised sheep. Each year there would be several lambs that had to be bottle fed because their mothers did not have enough milk or had disowned them. These lambs would become our pets. Once they were accustomed to the bottle, they would be at the gate immediately, waiting to be fed, each time you entered the barn.

The pet lambs would follow you around and even suck on your clothes because you had become a substitute mother to them. As they grew and were weaned from the bottle, they were still the friendliest sheep in the flock because they were not afraid of people. We had nourished them, and they remained faithful and loyal.

Sheep, though, can be one of the dumbest animals. A sheep can roll over onto its back and die, by cutting off all of its oxygen supply. It is not smart enough to roll back over and stand up. I remember one sheep dying like this on our farm. The old ewe did not have enough sense to turn back over.

Within a flock there is usually one sheep that is the leader. I am not sure how the leader is chosen, but the rest of the flock will follow their leader anywhere, even to their own doom. Sheep tend

148

to follow in a line and thus make a path in the field which they usually follow each day in the pasture.

Sheep also know the voice of their shepherd. Our sheep knew the voice of my dad and would follow him and come when he called to them. I remember trying to call the sheep, but they would not listen and only came when called by their shepherd, my dad.

One day my dad, brother and I were moving our sheep to a different pasture across the highway which divided our farm. Everything started out smoothly, but then something scared the leader, and she took off in the wrong direction with the flock close behind her. My dad called to the sheep and most followed my dad's voice, but not the leader. She took off across the plowed fields with several sheep close behind her. My brother and I took off running after the sheep. They did not listen to our voices as we called to them since we were not their shepherd. After running for what seemed miles, the sheep turned around after hearing again the voice of my dad who kept calling for them. They ran back to join the flock in their new green pasture.

Jesus tells us that He is our Good Shepherd. He calls for us to follow Him through the fields of our lives. All the fields will not be smooth and green. Some will be rough and rocky, but Jesus promises to be with us through each field and even carry us sometimes when we cannot go on.

To anyone who knows sheep, Jesus' comparison of us to sheep is appropriate. In our lives there are many people who want to be our leaders, but we need to know and recognize the voice of our leader and Shepherd, Jesus. Even when we know the voice of the Good Shepherd, there are times when other things or people distract us and we run away from the One who cares the most for us. But God continues to call to us, continues to seek us out, waiting for us to come home to the green pastures He has prepared for us.

**Prayer**

Good Shepherd, thank You for watching over me and calling me to follow. Guide me to follow Your leading and to listen to Your voice. Forgive me when I stray from You. Thank You for always welcoming me back with open arms. Amen.

# In His Arms

**Scripture**
**And Jesus took them (the children) in his arms and blessed them, laying his hands upon them.** - Mark 10:16

**And Jesus took a child, and put him in the midst of them; and taking him in his arms, he said to them, "Whoever receives one such child in my name receives me; and whoever receives me, receives not me but him who sent me.** - Mark 9:36-37

**It is the Spirit himself bearing witness with our spirit that we are children of God...** - Romans 8:16

I held his still, lifeless body in my arms. He was wrapped in a warm hospital blanket, but its warmth could not warm his cold body. Surrounded by his mother, father and grandparents in this sterile hospital delivery room, I said these words,

"Jonathan Cody, I baptize you in the name of the Father, and the Son, and the Holy Spirit. Amen."

Then I kissed his cold, blue forehead and gently laid him in the arms of his mother whose eyes were filled with tears.

Birth. It is supposed to be a time of joy and celebration as a new life is given as a gift from God. Most of the time it is, except when the child is born dead. Jonathan Cody was a still-born baby, the second stillborn his mother had bore. I was their minister and was called to the hospital after the parents were told the baby was already dead in the womb. The family asked if I would baptize their baby after he was born.

As I held this precious child in my arms, my heart cried for this child who was never given a chance at this life, he would

150

never walk, never throw a ball, never jump in a mud puddle, never go to school, never hug his parents, never ..... I held him in my arms and cried, which was all I could do, all anyone could do. Words were not necessary nor were there any magical words to bring hope into this hopeless situation.

I baptized this child not to assure that he would go to heaven for baptism is not a magical rite that opens the door to heaven.

God had already taken His angel to heaven. Baptism was more for the assurance of the parents that yes, their son was a child of God and was now given back to God.

Jonathan Cody left behind empty arms that longed to hold him, hug him and give to him all he needed and desired. Into the arms of God, Jonathan Cody went instead. We cannot explain the reason this beautiful baby was not given a chance at life. We just have the assurance he is with God.

Every time we share in a baptism, in a church, at a lake, or even in a hospital, God's loving arms are outstretched to receive His child and our promise of love, acceptance and responsibility.

Baptism is a sacrament of God's love expressing God's arms wrapped around us with His love, a love that will never let us go.

**Prayer**

Thank You, Lord, for the gifts of life, knowing we are forever in Your arms of love. Amen.

# Meal Time With God

**Scripture**

**Now as they were eating, Jesus took bread, and blessed, and broke it, and gave it to the disciples and said, "Take eat; this is my body." And he took a cup, and when he had given thanks he gave it to them, saying, "Drink of it, all of you; for this is my blood of the covenant, which is poured out for many for the forgiveness of sins."** - Matthew 26:26-28

**And taking the five loaves and the two fish he (Jesus) looked up to heaven, and blessed, and broke and gave the loaves to the disciples, and the disciples gave them to the crowds. And they all ate and were satisfied.** - Matthew 14:19-20

"Supper is ready. Let's eat." Wonderful words that bring back a treasure full of memories. Throughout my childhood, my family always ate our evening meal together no matter what we were doing or where we were going. Living on a farm though, supper was not high priority when it came to planting and harvesting season. Supper always waited until Dad came in from the fields.

I remember family dinners on Sundays and holidays with the whole family sitting around our dining room table or at my Grandmother's house. It was hard to wait as a little kid until everything was on the table and the prayer of thanksgiving was spoken so I could eat all the delectable food, especially dessert.

Not all meals went smoothly in the Clinger household. Many times in waiting for Dad, the potatoes would get soggy, the vegetables would become wrinkled and the meat would be dry. Being a normal family, there would be an accident or two, someone would spill his or her milk, someone would drop a spoon.

I remember the time my brothers were fighting at the table and kicking each other under the table. They kicked one of the legs of the table, and the leg broke. All the dishes and food went flying and crashed on the floor. After this incident, one brother had to sit at a small table by himself for weeks, and Mom bought plastic dinnerware.

As you read these words, I am sure memories have filled your mind of special meals in your own life, the big Thanksgiving Dinner with the entire family, your first candlelight dinner with the one you love, the last meal you ate with your parents before they went to God's banquet table.

Your memory is filled with some very exciting and memorable meals, while other meals were disasters that you would like to forget. The importance of meals is not so much the food, for sometimes it is hard to remember what you ate, but you usually remember with whom you ate and the special occasion. Eating is what brings us together so that we can share together in a more relaxed atmosphere. It is hard to eat with someone without talking with him/her and getting to know him/her.

Eating is something we all have in common. Therefore when Jesus fed the five thousand people in the Gospels, we can relate to the people who were hungry. They were hungry for food, but Jesus gave them food for their souls, too. Jesus gave them communion.

Communion, the Lord's Supper, is a meal where God's family gathers to remember Christ's death for us, to celebrate Christ's life among us and to go forth and share His love. It is a sacred and special meal.

We do not remember every time we have taken communion. We have held the bread and cup in church, at camp, in a hospital, in our home, and even on a mountainside. We have eaten a meal with Jesus each time, and while we do not remember each meal, we remember with whom we ate, Jesus Christ.

Every time we eat the bread and drink from the cup it is special, though some are more significant because of the surroundings, the event or the feelings and emotional need within us. We need to take communion as often as possible to be fed spiritually.

"Take, eat, this is my body. Drink. This is my blood."

## Prayer

Heavenly Father, thank You for food that gives nourishment to our bodies. May we nourish our souls and spirits, too, through Your Son's sacrifice and love. Amen.

# This Cup Is For You

**Scripture**

**In the same way also the cup, after supper, saying, "This cup is the new covenant in my blood. Do this, as often as you drink it, in remembrance of me."** - I Corinthians 11:25

**And he took a cup, and when he had given thanks he gave it to them saying, "Drink of it, all of you...."** - Matthew 26:27

I have a favorite cup in which I drink my hot tea, hot chocolate and hot lemon water. It was given to me by a friend several years ago. The cup has little pandas on it and says "It's always pandamonium around here!" I used to use it in my office and the saying seemed to be very appropriate.

The cup was given to me as a friendship gift, no special occasion, just a friendly, unexpected but thoughtful gift. By now the cup just has sentimental value.

By having a favorite cup, I know there is always a cup for me. I, somehow through the cup, know I belong here. I have my cup here.

When we come to the communion table there is always a cup for us. Whether there is one chalice and we drink out of it or dip our bread into it or whether there are small cups in which we partake of the juice, there is always a cup for us.

Even when we do not come to communion, there is still a cup waiting just for you. We are always welcome at the table. God waits for us to come, to give to us the cup, wanting us to share in the blood of Jesus Christ given to us out of love for us.

Now that I think about it, my panda cup is my second favorite cup. The communion cup is my favorite. The specialness is not in the cup itself but in the Giver of the cup. Jesus Christ gave His life just for me, just for you. It was a gift so unexpected and

155

thoughtful. He gave His life so we would be forgiven of our sins and given a new life.

The next time  you hold the  communion cup in your hands, whether the small cup or you touch the large chalice, know that this is your very own special cup of love given just because God loves you.  Now that's quite the cup!

**Prayer**

Lord, as I drink from the cup of Christ, I accept Your gift of love and ask for forgiveness of my sins.  Thank You, Lord, for the cup. Amen.

# Precious Memories

Scripture
**Beloved, we are God's children now; it does not yet appear what we shall be, but we know that when he appears we shall be like him, for we shall see him as he is.**      - I John 3:2

**Draw near to God and he will draw near to you.**      - James 4:8

Our lives are filled with precious memories of very simple yet profound events that have given direction and guidance for our lives. Think back in your life. What memories come to mind as precious? They can be the most common everyday event that takes on special significance because of the people involved and how it has stayed within your heart and memory.

One very precious memory for me is of my Grandfather Tewell. I always wanted to have a grandfather who would hold me in his lap, tell me stories and spoil his granddaughter. Unfortunately for me, my Grandfather Clinger died six years before I was born, and I have only one memory of my other Grandfather before he died. Therefore, this memory has become precious for a little girl who dreamed of having a grandfather.

I was about six years old. It was a warm summer morning in June. My Grandfather Tewell was visiting with us for a few days. I do not remember how long he was there, but I do remember that he stayed in our home. It was the week of Bible School and my brother, sister and I were preparing to leave for the morning. As our neighbor stopped in front of our house to take us to Bible School, I walked out the front door of our home and there sat my grandfather on the front porch in our white wooden lawn chair.

I remember looking at him. He smiled and waved good-bye. I do not remember any words being spoken, but I am sure we said good-bye. In my mind, I can still see his gray hair and his frail

157

body, but when I try to picture his face, all I see is the image of his smile.

Every time I recall this memory, it becomes more real to me and precious. I feel blessed to remember, and my grandfather comes alive for just a few minutes to love his granddaughter.

God grants to us precious memories which become holy, sacred moments when God reveals to us His love and grace. God comes to us in the ordinary events of our lives, and when God touches earth it becomes a sacred moment.

Within Christ's Church, we experience the sacraments of baptism and communion which are composed of the simple things of life - water, bread, and juice. To the outside world these are just ordinary substances of the earth, but to you and me they are sacred, precious moments because God has touched our lives in Jesus Christ through these simple elements.

There are many sacred moments or precious moments of our lives. Whenever God comes down and touches our lives and we receive a glimpse of God, then that moment is sacred.

God touches our lives more than we realize. Be open to the glimpses of God through the simple, yet precious moments and events of your life.

**Prayer**

Heavenly Father, You have come to earth through Your Son, Jesus, and continue to touch earth with Your love and grace. May I be open to Your touchings of my life. Amen.

# The Burden of Ministry

**Scripture**
**... appoint elders in every town as I directed you...** - Titus 1:5

**So I exhort the elders among you, as a fellow elder and a witness of the sufferings of Christ as well as a partaker in the glory that is to be revealed. Tend the flock of God that is your charge....** - I Peter 5:1-2

**These they set before the apostles, and they prayed and laid their hands upon them.** - Acts 6:6

**"And the disciples were filled with joy and with the Holy Spirit."** - Acts 13:52

From the moment I accepted the call of God into ordained ministry, I anticipated my ordination service. I had attended Annual Conference of the United Methodist Church at Lakeside, Ohio, since I was a youth. The ordination service at Annual Conference was always the high point of the week, and I knew one day I would be the one ordained.

The week finally arrived when I would be ordained Elder in the United Methodist Church. The week was filled with anticipation, excitement and a sense of awe. On the morning of ordination, June 11, 1986, the Bishop spoke to all the new Elders at a breakfast in our honor.

The Bishop talked about the "burden of ministry" given to us through the "laying on of hands." That evening as I was ordained and received the "laying on of hands" by two Bishops, I felt the weight of their hands on my head. I thought about the "burden of ministry" that had just been placed upon me. As they lifted their hands, I felt the release of the "burden" knowing I was not alone

159

in ministry. I knew God had given to me His Holy Spirit to carry me through the "burdens" and guide me in my ministry.

We are all called by God to minister to the world. A few are set apart for a specialized ministry as leaders. God gives to each of us the "burden of ministry." That is, He gives to us the responsibility of sharing His love, grace and mercy with others, and to be Christ's representatives in a hurting and needy world.

The "burden of ministry" is a heavy burden to bear, especially if we have to carry it alone. God has not called us to carry it alone. God has given to us His Holy Spirit to be always with us, to guide us and to carry us.

You are called. You do not go out alone. The Holy Spirit is with you. Accept your call to minister to God's children today.

**Prayer**

Thank You, Lord, for the gift of Your Holy Spirit that walks with us. Guide me in my "burden of ministry" to be always willing to serve You faithfully. Amen.

# The Back Pew

**Scripture**
**Therefore, since we are surrounded by so great a cloud of witnesses....** - Hebrews 12:1

**...because we have heard of your faith in Christ Jesus and of the love which you have for all the saints, because of the hope laid up for you in heaven.** - Colossians 1:4-5

**To the church of God which is at Corinth, to those sanctified in Christ Jesus, called to be saints together with all those who in every place call on the name of our Lord Jesus Christ, both their Lord and ours...** - I Corinthians 1:2

It was the smallest pew in our little country church though it held a prominent place in the back of the church just as you walked inside the swinging doors. Every child longed to sit in this seat of privilege, but every child knew it was reserved for two patriarchs of the church. There was never a "reserved" sign placed on the pew nor were there ever words spoken that it was reserved for a select few. Everyone just knew.

They walked into the church and calmly sat in their pew, two old gentlemen with gray hair, a farmer's tan (a white forehead where their hats had been) and dressed in their Sunday best. There they sat, singing in their beautiful bass voices the familiar old Gospel hymns and sometimes even talking over the preacher's voice. They were pillars of the church and the community.

Eventually, though, the two men died, but the pew remained for awhile. Some children sat in it, but it was not the same. Finally the pew was removed to make more room in the entrance way of the church, but the spirit of the men who sat in that back pew remains in that old Methodist Church even today.

161

Many saints have gone on to the world triumphant, but their spirits remain in the memories, hearts and walls of churches around the world.

Think for a moment of the saints of your church. Some you may personally remember because they touched your life and others you have just heard about by their names being spoken in reverence by others. The memory and deeds of the saints live on and help guide the church today.

Ministry is not nameless people, programs or buildings, but people, the saints of God. It is through those who sit in "the back pew" we get a glimpse of God. These saints walk with God daily, and if we will but listen to and observe their lives, we too, can receive a glimpse of God through them.

**Prayer**

God, thank You for the saints who have gone on before us. May we listen and learn from them as we see You in their faith. Amen.

Chapter 9

# Influences In Our Lives

*"May God bless you with good health and peace and increasing faith."*

*— Grandma*

*"She was very depressed or sad, so I tried to cheer her up too. At the same time I forgot my loneliness, and am thankful for all my blessings."*

*— Grandma*

*"I don't go on trips anymore or spend much on clothes now, so I think of helping others more now."*

*—Grandma*

# Nicknames

**Scripture**
**O Lord, thou hast searched me and known me!** - Psalm 139:1

**For all who are led by the Spirit of God are sons of God.**
- Romans 8:14

**Therefore the Lord himself will give you a sign. Behold, a young woman shall conceive and bear a son... and shall call his name Emmanuel.** - Isaiah 7:14

**... and he called his name Jesus.** - Matthew 1:25

We are given a name at birth before anyone knows who we really are or what we will become. It is our family name. We are usually given three names, some people more, some only two names. Our last name is usually our family name, the last name of our father. Now the other names can also be family names, named after a grandparent or other relative. Sometimes the name comes from a friend, a neighbor, or even a favorite character on television. Other times the parents just like the sound of the name. But wherever the name originates, it is our name as soon as it is spoken by our parents and officially typed on our birth certificate. Some people as adults change their name, but they are still known by their original name to some person.

Now as we grow and develop our personality, we may be given other names, nicknames. These names come usually from friends and family members because of what we do, how we look, of whom we remind them or just a pet name given out of loving affection.

We all have some type of nickname whether we admit it or not. It may be a mispronunciation of your name as a child that stuck; when you became a parent it is "Mom" or "Dad" or when you became a grandparent, "Grandma" or "Grandpa" or some variation. As a spouse, it may be an affectionate term like "Honey," "Darling," or "Sweetheart." Now these are names based on the love relationship.

When I was in eighth grade, one of my favorite T.V. shows was *Hogan's Heroes*. My group of girlfriends enjoyed the show, too, and soon we all took on the names of the characters of the show.

My nickname became "Colonel Klink" since my last name was "Clinger." That name stayed with me through the entire year of school.

When I was a junior in high school, I began playing on the tennis team. The tennis courts were next to the football practice field. To say the least, I was not a great tennis player and often hit the ball over the fence. The football coaches would throw the ball back over the fence, and after watching me practice for several weeks, the head football coach began calling me "Lefty" since I was left-handed. The nickname stuck. I even used that nickname to run for office my senior year in the Government Day elections with the slogan, "Put the Right One in Office, Vote for Lefty."

Then I began my first Pastorate about the time the show *M*A*S*H* was popular. Since my last name was Clinger, the Senior Minister's older son began calling me "Corporal" for Corporal Klinger on the show. The name stayed with me while serving the church, and there are still a few from the church who call me "Corporal" to this day.

There was one gentleman in the same church who had never been around a woman minister and did not frequent the church worship service though he was a good Christian man. After I became acquainted with several of his daughters, grandchildren and his wife, I finally met Kenny. As soon as I was introduced to him, he called me "Pastorette." He said that he could not call me "Pastor" because I was a woman. Kenny called me "Pastorette" until the day he died.

A nickname should not be a negative term, though some people use names that degrade and hurt people. To me a nickname is a term of affection. It is a name given to someone you love for whom you care deeply. You would not bother giving a nickname to one for whom you did not have strong feelings.

God knows us by name. God calls us affectionately by the name He has given us, His Children. We are not strangers to a God who does not care about us enough to know our names. God knows us personally and so deeply that He calls us His very own, His beloved Children.

Jesus, after being with his disciples for three years, said to them,

"No longer do I call you servants, for the servant does not know what his master is doing, but I have called you friends for all that I have heard from my Father I have made known to you" (John 15:15).

Jesus knew his disciples intimately and called them friends. Jesus knows us and calls us friends. We have a Heavenly Father who knows us by name, who knows us so fully and intimately that He calls us by a special name, "My Child." We are not strangers to God. Therefore we, like Jesus, can call on the Father personally, saying, "Abba, Father."

**Prayer**

Abba, Father, You know me and You love me. Thank You. Amen.

# What's Your Name?

**Scripture**
**And he said to him, "What is your name?" And he said, "Jacob." Then he said, "Your name shall no more be called Jacob, but Israel...."**                      - Genesis 32:27-28

**I therefore... beg you to lead a life worthy of the calling to which you have been called.**                      - Ephesians 4:1

**...to lead a life worthy of the Lord, fully pleasing to him, bearing fruit in every good work and increasing in the knowledge of God.**                      - Colossians 1:10

**To this end we always pray for you, that our God may make you worthy of his call, and may fulfill every good resolve and work of faith by his power...**                      - 2 Thessalonians 1:11

When my husband, Dave, was a young boy, his dad and mom instilled in him the importance of his name. His parents would say to him, "You are a Sturtz. Whatever you do reflects on our family. If you do good, we all enjoy your success. If you do wrong, we all suffer as a family. Son, be proud of who you are."

Dave continues to instill the value of the Sturtz name in his grandsons. "What's your name?" Dave will ask Christopher and O'Shay. After they respond with their names, Dave tells them, "Always remember who you are and be proud of your name."

What is so important about a name? We all have a name which sets us apart from others and gives us our identity. When a name is spoken an image appears in our minds of the person along with an emotional feeling toward the person. Some names command immediate respect and importance like an old commercial for a brokerage firm: "When _____ speaks, people listen."

169

Dave has an uncanny gift for remembering people's names and always something about them. He may not have seen the person for 20 years, but he still remembers his or her name and asks, "How's your back doing? Do you still have that little dog?" And the person is always surprised first of all that Dave remembers him or her and that he remembers something about his or her life.

Do you remember names? I try very hard to associate people with their names and where I met them. When I was introduced to the Staff Parish Committee at St. Paul's United Methodist Church in Celina, I sat in a room of about 25 people who introduced themselves and their spouses to me and told of their involvement in the Church.

After the introduction, a comment was made that it would take some time to get to know everyone in the Church even in this room. Someone jokingly said, "You seemed to pay attention when we introduced ourselves. Can you tell us our names?" Immediately, I went around the circle and named all the people. They were impressed to say the least.

But the key is listening. When you meet new people, you need to listen to their name, repeat their name and talk with them by name. Listening expresses that you care about them and by calling them by name, you convey to them that they are important and impart to them respect and honor.

Do you think God remembers names? Of course God does, and God remembers each one of us personally and remembers all the big and little things about you. We are to be proud of who we are, the children of God. We are to be proud of our name, Christians.

God calls us by name and wants us to live up to the high standards of our name. Paul tells us in Ephesians, "Lead a life worthy of the calling to which you have been called" (4:1). We have been called by God to be His disciples in this world, leading a life worthy of this calling. You are worthy because you have been chosen and accepted in the eyes of God.

You are called to lead a life worthy of your name. You are a child of God. You are a Christian. Whatever you do reflects upon the entire family, the entire Christian family of God. Be proud of your name.

170

**Prayer**

Heavenly Father, I am Your child. Thank You for calling me and loving me. May I always be proud of who I am because of Your love for me. Amen.

# The Extravagance Of Love

**Scripture**
**Mary took a pound of costly ointment of pure nard and anointed the feet of Jesus and wiped his feet with her hair; and the house was filled with the fragrance of the ointment.**

- John 12:3

**So we know and believe the love God has for us. God is love, and he who abides in love abides in God, and God abides in him.** - I John 4:16

When I turned 25 years old, I received my first teddy bear for my birthday from the church secretary. Now this may seem like an unusual gift for a minister in her twenties, but to me it was the perfect gift. I had mentioned to Mary that I had never had a teddy bear while growing up and felt like I had missed out on a precious childhood memory.

I immediately hugged my new teddy bear, and I knew instantly he was to be my special friend. I proudly rode home on my bicycle holding my new treasure with no thought of what people would think. My teddy bear slept in my bed for years, and I knew that I was not alone when he was there. He would always love me, and I could hold him and hug him whenever I wanted.

But there is a limit to the love a teddy bear can give just as there are limits to most things in our world. Each day we drive our car we see the speed limit signs, and when we do not obey the limit there can be the consequence of a speeding ticket. When we pour water into a glass there is a limit to how much it will hold before it runs over. There are limits to our credit cards, our stomachs, and sometimes our patience.

Everything in this world has limits except for one, love. Love has no limits, especially when it is God's love. God always loves us, and His love is overflowing and never runs out and is always unconditional. God is our shelter and our place of security and safety. God loves you.

As adults we cannot carry our teddy bears into the world, and even if we did their love would not be enough to face the burdens, problems and needs in our lives. We outgrow the usefulness of teddy bears for we know they cannot love us back. They will grow ragged and fall apart, but God's love will never grow old. God's love is a love that will not let us go.

God's love is an extravagant kind of love. God gives in excess. That is, we can never use up God's love nor will God withhold his love because of our sin. Therefore, there should never be a time when you say, "Nobody loves me. I feel so unloved." For that is not true. God always loves you and never stops loving you no matter what you have done, no matter who you are. You are loved.

**Prayer**

God, thank You for always loving me. I love You. Amen.

# The Prodigal

**Scripture**
**Not many days later, the younger son gathered all he had and took his journey into a far country, and there he squandered his property in loose living. And when he had spent everything, a great famine arose in that country, and he began to be in want.**                                                  - Luke 15:13-14

**Truthful lips endure forever, but a lying tongue is but for a moment.**                                                  - Proverbs 12:19

**Hatred stirs up strife, but love covers all offenses.**
                                                  - Proverbs 10:12

Lord, he said he would be here, but he never came. He said he would bring the money, but he did not. He said he would take care of the place, but he does not. He said there is nothing to worry about, that he has everything under control, but he does not. He lies to us every time. He frustrates us to the point of wanting to give up, but we love him. What he does and does not do brings anger into our lives, and we loose control and take it out on one another. Lord, what should we do?

Lord, You are a Father. How can You love us, care for us and help us, when we sometimes do the very same things to You? We promise to follow You, but we do not. We say we will give to You and to Your children in need, but we take care of ourselves and forget our promise to You. We lie to You. We come to You when we are only in need. You bail us out, and then we forget our promise to abide in Your presence and listen to Your guidance.

Lord, it is so frustrating when we try to help another, but feel like we are being used. He takes no responsibility for his life and his daily living. What if we stop helping him? Could we live with the guilt if something happened? How far are we supposed to go? Is there a limit to helping?

Lord, there is no limit to Your love. You love us unconditionally even when we take no responsibility for what happens in our lives and even blame You for our problems and sorrow. Lord, how can You love without limits and without any strings attached? Teach me, Lord.

How do you deal with this, Lord? Does Your heart break because of us, too? Lord, do You cry tears over me? Lord, I know You understand my feelings and the sorrow in my heart. Thank you Lord for listening and for always being here for me and loving me.

**Prayer**

Lord, forgive me when I limit Your love by not allowing it to flow through me to others. Forgive me. Amen.

# Coach

**Scripture**
**But the Lord said to Samuel, "Do not look on his appearance or on the height of his stature, because I have rejected him; for the Lord sees not as man sees; man looks on the outward appearance, but the Lord looks on the heart."**   - I Samuel 16:7

I received a phone call from my brother telling me that Mr. Neiswander had died. I had not seen him in over 16 years, nor thought about him much since high school. Mr. Neiswander had been my chemistry teacher for two years.

My memory kicked into gear and thoughts filled my mind of "Coach." Coach was not really a coach. He had never coached a sports team, but everyone called him "Coach" though I do not remember why now.

He was a small old man even when I had him for a teacher. Coach always wore his long white lab coat over his shirt and tie. His hair was buzzed and some days he did not shave. Most of the boys were much bigger than Coach, but Coach was an intimidating man. He always talked in a low mumble that was hard to understand.

Coach was a rough-looking and rough-talking man, but he was really a kind, sensitive man. His first wife had died only two or three years before I had him as a teacher. You could tell he missed his wife and missed the care of a woman. He enjoyed teaching teenagers and the company they provided for a lonely old man. Once you got to know Coach, which most kids who took two years of chemistry did, you really liked him.

In chemistry class Coach loved experiments, and we did them all the time. Once I poured sulfuric acid into an experiment, and it blew up all over my wrist. Coach immediately took charge of the situation with baking soda and cold water. I still have a small scar on my arm as a reminder. Each time I look at the scar I think of Coach.

I became a friend to Coach and an assistant for him. I graded his papers and took care of his grade book. One of the last grading periods when Coach put my grade on my grade card, he looked at my grades and then apologized for giving me my only "B."

According to the world, Coach was nothing to look at and would not have been considered an ideal teacher for teenagers, but my classmates enjoyed Coach and learned more than chemistry from him.

For me, I learned to look beyond outside appearances and to the heart. For God looks at our hearts, not our physical appearance. Coach had a heart of gold. He would do whatever he could to help a student. He looked and, at first, acted like a mean old man, but once you took the time to know him, he was gentle as a lamb.

There are a lot of people in this world with rough edges but who have gentle hearts and spirits. We need to look beyond those rough edges and see the hearts of the persons as God sees them and love them by taking the time to get to know the real persons inside.

## Prayer

Lord, help me to look beyond outward appearances and see within another what You see, their love and their needs. Amen.

# Chapter 10

# A Vessel Of The Lord

*It's not the work I do*
*for which I am paid*
*that brings contentment*
*But the work I do*
*for which I give and receive love*
*That means the most*
*Assures me my heart*
*is at home with God.*

— *Elaine J. Sturtz 1992*

# Being An Influence On Others

**Scripture**
**Examine yourselves, to see whether you are holding to your faith. Test yourselves.** - 2 Corinthians 13:5

**For we are his workmanship, created in Christ Jesus for good works, which God prepared beforehand, that we should walk in them.** - Ephesians 2:10

**Therefore be imitators of God, as beloved children. And walk in love...** - Ephesians 5:1-2

**So, being affectionately desirous of you, we were ready to share with you not only the gospel of God but also our own selves, because you had become very dear to us.** -1 Thessalonians 2:8

We all wonder from time to time if we are making any difference in the world and in the lives of people around us. We wonder if our life is expressing the love of Christ to anyone. We would like an opportunity like George in the movie, "It's A Wonderful Life" to see what would have happened if we had not been born to assure us that we are influencing others for the good. We may plant a seed of faith in someone and never see it develop roots. We may water the faith and never see it blossom. But that is what God calls us to do, to be faithful and share His love and grace no matter the results.

Sometimes we are given a glimpse of what we have done that has made a difference in the lives of others. When I moved from Marysville to serve a church in Cincinnati, the youth of the church wrote their good-byes in a book that was presented to me before I left. As I read and even today re-read these words, tears of thankfulness and humility fill my heart and flow down my cheeks. God gave to me a glimpse of hope that I was doing His work through simple acts of love.

Here are a few quotes from the youth of Marysville:

"You've taught me some important things about life."- Chris

"You have shown me how to grow with Christ and helped me to understand that no matter what He will always be with me." - Missy

"You have led me to Christ! I have seen so many times through you how Christ is a part of my life. How He can bring guidance, friendship and love, and I learned this from you." - Kelly

And later in a letter from one of the youth:

"You planted the seed of God's love in my heart. You helped me to see that being a Christian can be fun. You allowed me to be me. For all of this and so much more, I thank you for serving the Lord." - Connie

I share these words from the youth in humbleness of how God used me to touch the lives of these youth. Most of the time you never know if what you have done or said has brought anyone closer to Christ.

Who has influenced your life? I have shared of the profound influence my grandmother had on my life, and I told her many times personally. Though she never read my first book, *Love Lighted Path*, she knew about the book. It was written to express how my Grandmother influenced my life.

Why not tell the people who have influenced your life about how they have done so, not to give them recognition, for most people who are influences do not seek recognition, but to let them know that they are making a difference in their corner of the world.

No matter who we are or how humble we are, we all have our times of doubt and wondering if we are really doing God's will and work on earth.

**Prayer**

Heavenly Father, I strive to live following Your will. May others see Christ in my life and follow Christ. Amen.

# All In The Family

**Scripture**
**And he will turn the hearts of fathers to their children and the hearts of children to their fathers....** - Malachi 4:6

**See what love the Father has given us, that we should be called children of God; and so we are.** - I John 3:1

**Children, obey your parents in the Lord, for this is right. Fathers, do not provoke your children to anger, but bring them up in the discipline and instruction of the Lord.**
- Ephesians 6:1, 4

For the first 18 years of my life, I lived with my parents on the same farm and lived the same basic routine all those years. My three brothers and one sister were a vital part of those years, though they did not always live under the same roof. We would visit quite often with many of our relatives and attend family reunions each year.

A family. Most of us have a family, but not all of us had a wonderful family life. Some people never talk with their family once they move out of the family home, and others may see each other often but never really know one another.

Why is it so hard for some families to share their feelings and love for one another? When I was on my Emmaus Spiritual Renewal weekend, I received a letter from my mom which read in part: "It seems there are a lot of things I would like to say but just never do. I am sure you know we love you and are back of you 100%."

These words written touched my heart and opened the door of tears and a closer relationship. Sometimes it takes a special event or time of sorrow to bring these feelings into words.

185

God created us to live together as a family, and God intended that it was in the family we would learn about Him and develop our faith. But many times, it is in the family unit that we tend not to live out our faith. It is to our family we should express our faith the most, but we sometimes treat the ones we love the most the worst by not expressing God's forgiveness or mercy.

The faults of family members and even co-workers are magnified because you see them every day and the little things that they do become great annoyances. Therefore, we tend to be much more judgmental and less patient and unforgiving thus not expressing the faith that is within us. We tend to treat strangers better than our own family whom we love.

Communication is better between nations at war than it is in some families. Fighting and not speaking to one another becomes a natural way of family life.

Since moving away from home at eighteen to attend college, seminary and begin my career as a minister, I have encountered many family situations. I lived with several families during my school days, and also did a lot of baby-sitting for families. I am not an expert on family life, but I have encountered a wide variety of experiences.

It is within the confines of family life that we are truly ourselves with no reservations and no walls. It is here we try on new personalities, attitudes and styles like we try on clothes to see if they fit as we mature and develop into who we really are.

The key to family life is love. We need to tell each other, "I love you"; when we know love abides in the family, we can endure the growing pains and we can forgive the sins because love is present. The family needs to be centered on love, God's love; for without God at the center of any relationship there is no depth, no one to go to when the other has let you down.

This I have learned through experience, and not all of it has been pleasant. Marrying into an already-established family has been a growing and maturing experience. I have had to accept people as family although I had no part in their development or experiences. If God was not at the center of my life and our marriage, this would be virtually impossible.

**Prayer**

Heavenly Father, thank You for the gift of family. May I love and accept my family for who they are, Your beloved children. Amen.

# Steve And Troy

**Scripture**
**Other seed fell on good soil and brought forth grain some a hundredfold, some sixty, some thirty.** - Matthew 13:8

"Do you remember when we.....?" In a matter of a few months I had begun two conversations with these words as I shared some special moments with two young men who had been a vital part of the youth program in my first pastorate.

I received a wedding invitation from Steve, and joy filled my heart that he would want me to be present on this holy day of his life. The wedding was beautiful, and of course, I cried to see this boy, now a man, join his life with another in the bond of marriage.

Then I went back to Marysville for the Homecoming at the United Methodist Church and walking toward me was a good-looking young man.

He stopped and said, "Do you remember me?"

I said, "Troy!" and we hugged.

Steve and Troy! What a pair! It was a joy to see them again and to remember how God worked in our lives as we shared together in the life of the Church.

Steve and Troy were in my first Confirmation Class, actively involved in the total youth program of the Church, attended all the work camps, and were regular visitors to my office.

We grew up together essentially since I served their church as my first pastorate while still in seminary, and they had just become teenagers. To quote Steve from the note he wrote to me as I left Marysville, "Here's the story ... Confirmation Class, Beverly, McArthur, Coal Trucks, First Work Camp at Camp Otterbein, weed wacking, pulling cat tails. One time in Beverly, Red Bird Mission, Troy and I went into the woods with some guy about a mile off the main Road to an old lady's house to replace an oven and this was the SCUMIEST 'house' I'd ever been or ever seen some-one live in, but after leaving her 'house' it gave me a good sense of helping someone in need and also helped me realize and appreciate what items I have. I've learned alot of things through work camps and times just talking about life."

For five years I shared in the lives of these two boys and their families from performing the wedding of Steve's mother to his stepfather to baptizing Troy's niece, Erin. Steve and Troy also shared in the life of my family by helping me paint the barn on my parents' farm.

The parents of Steve and Troy were always amazed that their sons were willing to pay to go to Work Camp and that they actually worked at camp. Work Camp was more than just work, though we worked hard. It was about sharing God's love with others, accomplishing a task together while having a great time, developing friendships that would last forever, and truly being Christ's hands in the world.

We participated in many activities together. They were actively involved in the life of the church, even to the point of coming forward as teenagers for the Children's Sermon each Sunday I gave the sermon. The important part of our relationship was that Christ was in the center and together we grew in our relationship with Christ.

As I talked with Steve and Troy seven years later, it was evident that Christ was at the center of their lives and their marriages. God had used me as a vessel of His love to be a positive influence in the lives of two youth and had used two youth to be a positive influence in the life of their minister. Steve and Troy are now role models for other youth as they share Christ with others.

Sometimes we may wonder if we planted any seeds because we do not see the growth and fruit of our labor. Then there are those rare occasions that God allows us to see a glimpse of the fruit of our labor that reassures us that we are on the right path toward God.

**Prayer**

Thank You, Lord, for people who walk with us for awhile on our journey of life. May we be open to Your seed planting. Thank You for the glimpses of growth You allow us to see. Amen.

# Shared Faith Of Blackbirds

**Scripture**
**Look at the birds of the air: they neither sow nor reap nor gather into barns, and yet your heavenly Father feeds them. Are you not of more value than they?**           - Matthew 6:26

**Jesus said to them, "I am the bread of life; he who comes to me shall not hunger, and he who believes in me shall never thirst."**                               - John 6:35

From my kitchen window I watched the blackbirds slowly fly under the apple tree, land and walk regally toward the stale bread I had spread on the ground just minutes before.

One blackbird took a piece and flew away. Another took a bigger piece and slowly walked a few yards, while the third blackbird walked toward the bread but did not pick up any but flew away with the second bird into the yard next door.

As I watched, the first blackbird was eating his piece of bread but the second bird landed next to the third blackbird and shared his bread with her.

I wondered why, when there had been plenty of bread under the apple tree for all three birds to have their own, the second blackbird willingly shared his bread with the third and why the third blackbird did not take any herself

As I sat down at the kitchen table to ponder this, God spoke to my heart. Are you willing to share what you have even when there is an abundance for all?

There are people in this world who cannot take bread by themselves. They need someone to give it to them and show them the way.

How much like our faith are these birds. Some easily accept the gift of love and salvation given by God, while others see it but do not know how to receive it on their own. They need someone who will share it with them so that they may feed on the love and Word of God and thus fully accept the gift of salvation.

**Prayer**

Lord, guide me in sharing Your Bread of love with each person I meet today. Amen.

# A Vessel Of Hope

**Scripture**
**"O death, where is thy victory? O death, where is thy sting?"**
- I Corinthians 15:55

**"Let not your hearts be troubled; believe in God, believe also in me."** - John 14:1

My husband attended the funeral of a former State Trooper on a bitterly cold, dismal, wintery January day in a small Ohio town. The minister's words were as cold and frigid as the weather outside. He talked only of God's condemnation and judgment, telling those who were mourning that our lives are as bleak as the winter. He gave no words of hope and comfort, nor did he speak words of the good life of this Christian man. He talked only of pulling all our baggage of wrongs with us like a dog pulls the sled in the frozen tundra of the North.

The minister led those in attendance to believe life is futile, with no purpose and no hope of the eternal promise of heaven for those who follow Christ. It was a sad day in so many ways. My husband came home cold from the weather and from the words of this minister.

In contrast, I went to the funeral home for the time of visitation at the death of a distant relative and family friend. I had to stand in line waiting to express my sympathy to the family because so many people loved this man, and he had touched the lives of so many people. The family only talked of hope and love, knowing their loved one was now in heaven walking and talking with Jesus. There was sadness at our loss of such a wonderful Christian man here on earth, but there was joy that he was now in heaven.

Words of hope and assurance are needed at a time of loss; one needs to hear that God is a God of hope, love and mercy, not a God of judgment and condemnation. As Christians, a funeral is a time to celebrate the gift of this life and the entrance into the next life with God. Because of the death of Christ on the cross, we need not carry our baggage of sin into eternity. We are forgiven of our sin, and our slate is washed cleaned by the blood of Christ. We enter into heaven forgiven children of God.

**Prayer**

Heavenly Father, thank You for the hope of heaven that we may live forever with You as your forgiven children. Amen.

Chapter 11

# Poems

# Friends

God knows when we need a friend
bringing together two persons in need,
sharing a mutual pain
bearing soul to soul
words flowing easily into understanding heart.
When the brokenness took residence within me,
God reminded me there is someone coming,
allowing our paths to cross,
before needing one another,
thus allowing you to come in,
when the time was right.
Out of the depths of my soul
spilling out the blood
laying wounded and bleeding
only one who also hurt
saw the wounds
for you had an open scar,
Mutual hurt bonded our souls
without our minds accepting the change
quickly again the giving and sharing begins
giving though holding back,
risking though cautious
willing though apprehensive.
Soul Friends.

8/26/86

# Personal Awareness

God, You are real
    alive from the beginning which You created.
You fill the world with love
    but my sin covered Your love
    discoloring the brightness of the world
        staining lives forever.
I cannot deliver myself from sin
    which grips me firmly
    clinging to all that I have and am.
Make me see Your mercy
    shine it down upon me
        like the rays of the sun.
Let me be aware of Your gift of grace.
Awareness of my sin-sick soul
    occupies my thought and daily existence
    knowing only You can cleanse my soul
        from this burden of sin.
Personal awareness of Your power and grace
    seeing life through new lenses
        dimly, though, the picture fades.
Realizing You can change my life
    allowing me to see clearly
    my sin and my forgiveness.
New perspecitve changes attitude
    causing tides to flow in a new direction
    surrounding a new island of my life.
Aware of the simple and honest
    child-like faith is all You ask.
Coming to You as a child
    finding love, acceptance and new life.
Knowing I am a child of God
    who is loved and forgiven.
        1984

# Life Is A Conversion

Life is one conversion after another
    constantly changing, growing, progressing
Searching for meaning and reality
    finding hope and faith.
Walking in faith until faith is yours
    and your heart is God's.
Finding love, courage, strength
    to face the situations of life
Knowing you are surrounded and filled with
    life-giving power,
        the love of God through Jesus Christ.
Love that layed down its life, his death
    for me and for you,
        that we might live a life in His love.
Laying down my life
    that I might serve others
    dying in order to bloom
    dying a caterpillar and rising a butterfly.
For in God's love
    we die to the self, first accepting self
    as God's child with gifts, graces, talents
    using them in service to others and God,
        thus dying to selfishness
Finding life takes on new meaning
    when lived for God and for others.

                1984

# My Life

My life has been filled with the Christian way
    always being fed on God's Word
        through the Church and family,
    being fed but never fully nourished
        taking in the food
            but never extracting the needed vitamins
            to grow in my own faith,
    trying to feed on another person's faith.
Off to new horizons in search of myself
    finding new ways to feed
        turning away from the old
    thinking I've matured enough
        to handle my own life.
Feeding myself on the latest thought and ideas
    "I can do it on my own." I said.
    As I went under for the last time.
Realizing I was eating
    but not the food that gives spiritual growth.
As I looked back
    I saw the daily bread of living
        given to me by others,
        the love and care I received
        the laughter and the joy.
I saw Christ's hands stretch out
    waiting to give to me
    as I received.
        Christ gave so much
        that my eyes opened to give to others
    knowing Christ continues to give to me,
        to give love, strength, comfort.
Opening a new department in my life
    a department of sunshine and rainbows and butterflies
        hopes restored,
            spirits lifted,
                enthusiasn renewed.
For as I give, I receive.

1984

# I Am

I am a grain of sand
    in the endless beach of time.
I am a drop of water
    in the ocean of God's creation.
I am a special treasure
    God's unique shell on the shore of life.
I am a wave that beats upon the beach
    smoothing out the roughness
        of my life
    guided by the wind of the Spirit
        leaving treasures of untapped
           beauty and wonder;
    though pulling me under at times
    the current forces me gently to be anchored firmly
        in the One who keeps me from falling.
I am a vital part of God's creation
    the only one who can be and do
        what God created me to be and do.
I am God's precious child.

                         12/19/88